ADHD Treatment Approaches

How I Took Control

by
Jory Ames

ISBN-13: 978-1979931267
ISBN-10: 1979931267

Publisher: Wordsworth LLC Publishing
www.wordsworthwriting.net

To contact the publisher, e-mail: editor@wordsworthwriting.net. To contact the author, e-mail: jory@joryames.com.

This book is not intended to take the place of medical advice from a trained medical professional.

PREFACE

Thank you for sharing this ADHD exploration together with me!

I always kept in mind, while writing this, that — although I am sharing very personal stories — many people have similar issues in their lives and are also looking for answers.

First, I aimed to help others by being honest about my own experiences. Second, I wanted to do the following to help not just me but others with ADHD by doing the following:

- Research ADHD treatments and suggestions;
- Read books, articles, and websites;
- Try many of the suggestions; and
- Offer my feedback on what I've explored.

I hope this journal helped you know that you are not alone. I care about you and what you are struggling with.

Together, we can find the good in ADHD and make it work for us — to our advantage — instead of us feeling like ADHD is controlling our lives.

Overall, I think educating myself has been the most powerful tool of all. Understanding ADHD with both its gifts and challenges has made it easier for me to live with and, I think, easier for others to live with me.

Let us strive to enjoy this journey of self-discovery together.

AUTHOR'S NOTE ON READING

If you want to jump around, skim, or only read passages relevant to your own life, go ahead! Be free! Throw away the guilt!

As ADHDers, we've been told we have to start a book at page one and not stop till we've reached the end.

But we know other ways of reading sometimes work best for us.

Maybe you might read more than one book at once, picking up what you feel like that day.

Who told you that's not fine? Not me! And I used to teach college English.

This book is my gift to you. Read it as you wish, or don't read it at all. If, for example, in Treatment Approaches, you wish to skip some topics that don't interest you or that you already have a strong handle on, go for it!

Your book, your life, your choice.

Please, let go of thinking you are "bad" because a task is unfinished. Even though I provide guidance on how I finish tasks, that doesn't mean I'm going to complete all of my grand ADHD ideas before my life ends. Does it matter? Of course not.

Let us, most of all, rejoice in the beauty that is us ... as we are. And if in slipping into this book a little, you find you want to change something about yourself to make your life easier, that is entirely up to you.

You are unique and wonderful just the way you are.

CONTENTS

PART ONE:

LEARNING ABOUT ADHD & TREATMENT OPTIONS

1. My Treatment Approaches #1: Education

My mind is, as always, on a constant racetrack of ideas and concerns, although "racing" is a bad analogy for what ADHD feels like, unless it's a racetrack after a giant crash, with cars strewn everywhere, people running frantically around the wreckage, some injured bodies crawling, fire and smoke and screams ... *that* is what a "racing mind" feels like. Chaos.

Fun Times Ahead…The Three Subtypes of ADHD

First, we must take control by self-educating.

Fortunately, I love learning new things.

Even when they involve my brain.

So here's to a new adventure – learning about ADHD!

Don't worry, I'll keep it short and leave out all the detailed tests and definitions and doctor-speak. Let's have some fun instead, with a brief discussion of the three types of ADHD.

These days, ADHD is often separated into three subtypes. A person is either predominantly inattentive, hyperactive-impulsive, or combined (I am clearly the latter; I have it all!). Here are the symptoms of the subtypes ("Attention ... " *Wikipedia*).

Inattention

- Be easily distracted, miss details, forget things, and frequently switch from one activity to another
- Have difficulty maintaining focus on one task
- Become bored with a task after only a few minutes, unless doing something enjoyable
- Have difficulty focusing attention on organizing and completing a task or learning something new
- Have trouble completing or turning in homework assignments, often losing things (e.g., pencils, toys, assignments) needed to complete activities
- Do not seem to listen when spoken to
- Daydream, become easily confused, and move slowly

- Have difficulty processing information as quickly and accurately as others
- Struggle to follow instructions

Um, me me me me…. Although I am good at instructions and paying attention as long as its written, not oral. (However, I can't seem to bear to read instructions for equipment such as how to put together a treadmill or use a BlueRay player…does *anyone* read those things? When I taught, I'd bring them in to my technical writing classes so we could analyze what was wrong with them. Things like "put the screw in slot A," but they didn't say which screw, and there were 20 different types and sizes.)

Hyperactivity

Note: These hyperactivity symptoms tend to go away with age and turn into "inner restlessness" in teens and adults with ADHD.

- Fidget and squirm in their seats
- Talk nonstop
- Dash around, touching or playing with anything and everything in sight
- Have trouble sitting still during dinner, school, doing homework, and story time
- Be constantly in motion
- Have difficulty doing quiet tasks or activities

Um, me me me me….

Impulsivity

- Be very impatient
- Blurt out inappropriate comments, show their emotions without restraint, and act without regard for consequences
- Have difficulty waiting for things they want or waiting their turns in games
- Often interrupt conversations or others' activities

Um, me me me me….

I am so overwhelmingly ADHD!

Another Definition…My Favorite!

The definition of ADHD above, with the three subtypes, is standard nowadays, but I rather appreciate the detailed list in Hallowell and Ratey's 1994 opus: *Driven to Distraction*. This book, and its more recent companion, *Delivered from Distraction*, are worth delving into, but in the meantime, here are brief summaries of their "Suggested Diagnostic Criteria" for ADD in adults; I seem to have all of them, I'm proud to say:

1. *A sense of underachievement.*
2. *Difficulty getting organized.*
3. *Chronic procrastination or trouble getting started.*
4. *Many projects going simultaneously.*
5. *Tendency to say what comes to mind without necessarily considering the timing or appropriateness of the remark.*
6. *Intolerance of boredom.*
7. *Easy distractibility, trouble focusing attention, tendency to tune out or drift away in the middle of a page or a conversation, often coupled with an ability to hyperfocus at times.*
8. *Often creative, intuitive, highly intelligent.*
9. *Trouble in going through established channels, following "proper" procedures.*
10. *Impatient; low tolerance for frustration.*
11. *Impulsive, either verbally or in action, as in impulsive spending of money, changing plans, enacting new schemes or career plans, and the like.*
12. *Tendency to worry needlessly, endlessly; tendency to scan the horizon looking for something to worry about, alternating with inattention to or disregard for actual dangers.*
13. *Sense of insecurity.*
14. *Mood swings, mood changes, especially when disengaged from a person or project.*
15. *Restlessness.*
16. *Tendency toward addictive behavior.*
17. *Chronic problems with self-esteem.*
18. *Inaccurate self-observation.*
19. *Family history of ADD or manic-depressive illness or depression.*
20. *Childhood history of ADD.*
21. *Situation not explained by other medical or psychiatric condition.*

What an excellent jewel of a list! I can certainly see myself in most, if not all, of these. Can you?

Why I Love the Internet

My beloved godmother, who passed away last year, was concerned about the Internet and her granddaughters' exposure to it. Pretty much all she knew about it was what was on the nightly news – the Craigslist Killer, pedophiles stalking chat rooms, identify theft – those kind of things.

"No, it's wonderful," I said.

"Why?"

"Well, for one thing, I work at home. I don't have to go to an office like you did."

"I liked working in an office."

"I know you did. But I didn't. Now there's a choice for people like me."

"Oh, well, I still don't like it."

This conversation was probably 15 years ago.

The Internet has come a long way, baby, since then.

Especially in ways that help people with problems, such as ADHD.

First, you know you are not alone. There are online support groups and social media pages for whatever ails you.

Second, you can learn about your issue without moving from your seat. A wealth of information is out there, good and bad, and you just have to be smart enough to dissect it to find what is true and what isn't.

For example, I used to loathe *Wikipedia* and told my students to stay away – far away – from it. But I've come to respect it more and more as it's been shaped and reshaped by constant critical editors. Having a "live" encyclopedia at your fingertips is *awesome!* (Can you tell I'm the mother of a teenager?)

My sister has been, over the years, carefully mailing to my son, one at a time, the set of encyclopedias we had as children. She has taken so much time putting sticky notes inside beside each entry that should be meaningful to him, such as writing about our trip together under "Rome."

But he'll never look at it. I don't want to tell her that and break her heart. She's working so hard.

Those encyclopedias are from the 1960s! So much has been discovered and changed since then. Some of the countries in there don't exist anymore, and many countries have been formed since. I'm sure he'd scoff at what it says about the solar system, for example, since it's so outdated.

No, Corrin, children don't look at encyclopedias anymore. They look online. And that's okay, actually. I personally like to go to the Internet for information and support, both things I need with this ADHD issue.

Third, the Internet is never dull. An ADHDer can jump around from articles to personal experiences to pictures to jokes to lists of medication side effects to book reviews to brain scans to whatever. It's fantastic for someone with ADHD. It's especially fantastic when you have multiple monitors and can surf various sites at once. Good Lord. It's something I couldn't even have imagined as a child. (Maybe that very thing makes it worse for ADHDers; after all, when I was a child, I had no problem reading a novel right through to the end, but now I do.)

There's a fourth wonderful use of the Internet: practical, helpful tips on organizing, with photographs! How perfect for ADHDers. The only negative is that there are too many choices. So my purpose in this chapter is to summarize some of what I've learned that should be helpful to us, giving full links to referenced sites in the Works Cited section, in case you want to read more.

The main thing is to remember you are using the Internet. Don't let it use you, as in dominate your life and soul. Simply put: Limit your time spent on it.

If it's reading you want to do, consider getting an e-reader that does nothing else, or – remember these? – a book. (I can't tell you how many hundreds of times I've been reading a book on my iPad or phone when a message popped up that distracted me, or I distracted myself by looking something up, which led to me checking something else, which led to an app, which led to posting on Facebook, which led to ... not finishing the book!)

Learning about ADHD through Videos

The Internet provides easy access to ADHDers on symptoms, treatments, personal experiences, and current and past studies. If you prefer to watch videos rather than read, or just want to vary your approach, go to *YouTube* and type ADHD or Adult ADHD (or maybe something more specific like meditation and ADHD, staying focused, or organizing a closet). You'll find lots of glorious videos, some like dull college lectures, others hilarious, still others practical. In any case, you'll know, once again, that you are not alone!

Personally, I cannot watch videos at my desk. I not only get bored, but I feel like I'm wasting my time, and I'm distracted by work to do. I need to be in bed, at night, winding down, and then maybe I can pull them out on the iPad and watch.

Or, you could try what I just did, play a video (this on one staying motivated) in the background while doing a boring task (in this case, I was going through my file drawers finding and throwing away old tax receipts no longer needed). Win-win!

My son introduced me to "nigahiga," a young YouTuber, and if you want a laugh, watch his video, *How to Know If You Have ADHD*:

Source: Nigahiga

Reading Self-Help Books

I love reading self-help books for inspiration and ideas, especially people's personal stories. So throughout this year of self-improvement, making substantial changes in the little world that is my life, I have read numerous weight-loss and quit smoking books, and I managed to completely change my life in both those areas.

As part of my self-discovery journey, I have now been reading dozens of ADHD books and articles, building my knowledge, forcing myself to become an expert of sorts, at least in understanding myself and, I hope, finding solutions. In my case, my inattentive and impulsive behaviors are my main concern, as those affect others. Many of the other behaviors listed as ADHD I have applied various solutions to over the years, but I am open to other approaches, so I will summarize what I learn for you briefly in this section (as I know I don't have your attention for long, if you're at all like me!).

Just remember that reading self-help books is a great way to learn about ADHD and address your concerns.

The Best Thing I Learned: We Are Not Alone

The absolutely best thing I learned about ADHD is that I am not alone. ADHD is not a "personal failing" (Griffin), and there are many of us ADHDers out there. The web is filled with us, yammering away about our issues. So dive in, and enjoy yourself. Or grab a self-help book, and learn about yourself. Listen to an audio book in the car. Check Pinterest for organizing solutions or ADHD tips. Make learning about *yourself* a priority.

But, if you're not either (1) having fun, or (2) being educated, what's the point? Go play with the dogs instead. Visit someone – an actual person. Clean the sink. Whatever. Don't feel guilty or ashamed; just enjoy this special, precious life you've been given.

ADHD can considered a gift. ADHD children often have the following amazing characteristics (Honos-Webb in DeNoon):

- Creativity
- Exuberance
- Emotional expressiveness
- Interpersonal intuition
- A special relationship with nature
- Leadership

We are special – unique – in a good way.

I think we should change the definition of ADHD from "attention deficit hyperactivity disorder" to something positive and beautiful, maybe "always daydreaming, hoping, and daring"? Anyway, that's how *I'm* redefining it!

Where to Go for Support

Along the same vein of "we are not alone," I have learned that sharing my new-found knowledge can be freeing and actually help relationships. Some people won't listen and will pooh-pooh the diagnosis, and that's okay. But for others, it provides a window to your actions over your shared history together, reframed in a new, clearer, beautiful way, as if you scrubbed that blackened glass with Windex.

Here are some other ideas for where ADHDers can turn for support and acceptance, as well as tips to make our lives easier.

Self-Help Groups

To find out whether there is a local support group to help you climb through the branches of ADHD living, you can check online, such as at www.chadd.org. There are also online support groups, such as

- adhd.supportgroups.com
- www.chadd.org/Support/Virtual-Chapter.aspx
- www.ADDConsults.com
- www.MomsWithADD.com
- www.WomenWithADHD.com
- https://www.reddit.com/r/ADHD/

There are plenty more; these are just a few on Pinterest and the Internet. Search for what your special needs are, and you might just find the right group!

Social Media & Web Sites

I am not a wide user of social media, but there are numerous ADHD "feeds" and sites. One Facebook group, for example, is called ADHD Adult Support Group. I am sure there are Twitter and Instagram and every other kind of social medial sites for ADHDers. So whatever your favorite social media, explore a little if you wish, and find some support and humor in the situation.

I did check out Pinterest, and it was so full of ADHD pictures, jokes, posters, tips, and quotations that I got overwhelmed, but I realize it would be a great fun source when standing bored in line, so I created an ADHD pins list and saved that for another day. Looks like a great source of entertainment, if nothing else. (I also made a pin called "Organizing.")

Note: I don't quite understand Pinterest yet; it seems like clutter (and a lot of links to websites that want my money) to me, but I'm sure with some practice I could find it useful. Here is an example search and pictures: For this I typed "ADHD organization" in the top search bar. (I know it's unreadable, but it gives you an idea of what you'll see; then you click on a "pin" or box to go to that site. Like a typical ADHD web surfer, this is just one of the 12 tabs I had open on Chrome at the time, with my multitasking mind of a dozen things going at once. Sigh. You understand, don't you?

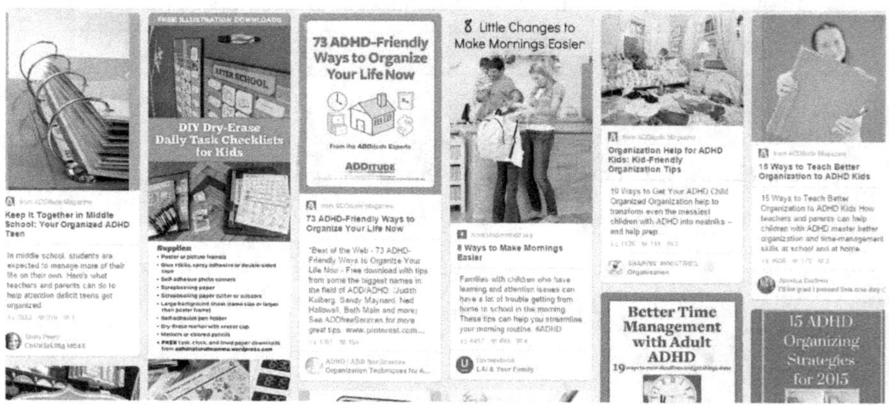

Or, if you're like me, and just don't want to add one more thing to your hectic schedule, then don't! No pressure!

Of course, the Internet is also filled with articles, groups, blogs, and videos about ADHD. So if you're more comfortable with exploring the Internet than creating social media (or, like me, get overwhelmed by too many social media accounts), then just type ADHD and see where the World Wide Web takes you.

Apps

I have tried a half-dozen or so free ADHD smart-phone apps. They vary in approach: tests, brain games, tips, and articles. New ones come out constantly, and there are also plenty of apps available that cost money, which I have not tried.

Other useful apps I have filed under folders on my iPhone as Secretary, Business, and To Do Lists. My favorites so far are Wunderlist (which I use for grocery and other shopping and errands – no more forgetting to pick up that one thing you needed at the store!) and my bank's online banking app (which I use for paying bills and depositing checks – no more driving to the bank!). There are also apps such as Scannable for scanning documents (really, it's just taking a picture, so now I do that anyway, and save them to the correct folder on my computer, such as my dogs' rabies records) and Itemize for itemizing receipts (it grabs them from your emails; you can also scan them).

Mostly, I am just exploring apps to learn whether there are a few to help me save time and stress. If you like apps, this might be good for you as well. Or just search online for "best apps for ADHD"; you'll find some great suggestions. A few that come up include:

- RescueTime
- Focus@Will
- Due
- EpicWin
- Clear
- Dragon Dictation
- Attention Exercise (a doodling app)
- Remember the Milk
- Task Timer
- Dropbox

Family & Friends

It amazes me how much nicer SO is being since I told him a little bit about my ADHD self-discovery project.

It's almost like he's a different person.

Or maybe I'm being a different person.

Whatever – we're not clashing so much. I don't think we've argued once in the week since I first told him, and that's incredible. We've been together for 19 years, and since my son was born 15 years ago, we've rarely gone a day without arguing.

Not serious, aggressive, evil, hateful, or threatening arguments. I've had those in other relationships. But mean enough to hurt.

I think he just needed an explanation. He always took my interrupting and distracted behaviors so personally. He thought it was a slap in his face. He thought I didn't like to listen to him.

"No SO," I explained, "I don't listen to anybody."

So sometimes, maybe it helps just to tell your loved ones.

Unfortunately, I haven't had much success talking to my siblings. We are an argumentative bunch of nay-sayers, trained by our mother to be skeptical of anything, which is probably why it took me years to get tested for ADHD and then years again to actually do anything about it.

But now, with my knowledge growing daily, I have wanted to share what I learned with my siblings. I've tried to tell two of them; they have been, frankly, disbelieving and generally negative about it, which was not unexpected. Maybe because I'm tossing out the theory that they might look into whether they also have ADHD, and raising the question of whether our mother did, upsets them. Too much to throw at a family at once. Let them think about it a little, push it to the back of their brains; let it slowly work its way back front, like it did with me, maybe even years from now, and perhaps their curiosity will overcome their fears.

My other sister, Ellen, the hoarder (and previously diagnosed with ADHD), was much more tolerant and interested. Surprisingly, I see she is going to be my best sounding board. She is also most aware of family history, as in generations of family. It's hard to reach her on a good day; I have to wait for her to call; that means she's physically and mentally able to talk. I am actually, for the first time in years, looking forward to our conversations. I just asked her to peruse her ADHD books with our relatives (mom?) in mind and let me know what she thinks. It was a nice conversation, and I'm looking forward to what I'm sure will be a thorough, detailed analysis, which she's good at once she has a project to focus on.

In any case, be prepared for friends and family to say, "No, you don't have that." Or, "That's ridiculous." Or, "That doesn't really exist." Keep trying. You'll find someone who understands.

Nature

A walk in the woods has always been my personal "medication" for my issues, long before I knew the name of this disorder was ADHD. When I walk my dogs in the woods, I find my mind calming. The exercise is good for my body; the woods are good for my soul.

And of course the dogs are ever-grateful.

I think more than anything, my best support has been my *self*. Being alone with myself in the woods, away from the computer, telephone, television, work, and just all the "stuff" of the world lets me relax.

Yes, there are many mornings that it is well below zero or windy as hell and I don't want to go. But even if it's just for a few minutes, I feel better if I do.

Rescue Dogs & Cats or Volunteer

I learned way back in high school, some 40 years ago, that when I became too inner-focused on my own sweet sorrows, I needed to step back and make a list of all the good things in my life. Then, I needed to take action, and volunteer for those less fortunate. In my case, usually that volunteer work involves animals, but whatever your passion is, follow it. Volunteering helps others while helping you – one of those win-win situations.

Not just volunteering, but adopting a pet helps me. Dogs and cats are loving, trusting, faithful, loyal, and nonjudgmental, which is amazing, considering what people put them through.

But notice I said "adopt" or "rescue." There's no need to encourage breeding when so many wonderful, adoptable pets are being killed (five million a year in the United States, alone).

Now, maybe I lost you here and you're mad at me because you breed dogs or cats. I don't really care. This the only place I don't care about you. Since high school, I have been volunteering for humane societies and animal controls, and I have seen too many perfectly beautiful souls killed, many just after being born, just because there aren't enough homes. So be mad. Then do something.

(I have a feeling that being obnoxiously opinionated might be a sign of ADHD. If so, I'm there!)

Go out and adopt a pet. If you work outside the home, get two, so they are not alone. If you're never had a pet, try to hang out with them a bit first. Maybe volunteer at your local animal shelter. Visit with friends who have pets.

But my dogs and cats have been the one stabilizing true love throughout my entire life. Their only flaw is that they have such short life spans. I have suffered terrible broken hearts when my dogs, particularly, have passed away. But I always tell myself, "There aren't enough homes for all the pets out there. You must rescue what you can. Yes, you will suffer when they die, but it is worth the love they give you during their lives."

This I tell myself, and this I believe.

Note: you must be patient with puppies. They will damage your house and your car. You will very possibly lose carpet, shoes, furniture, car seats, and much more to their messes and play. Personally, I accept this. I would never put a puppy in a crate all day, as many people do. I would never chain any dog outside. But there is a very easy solution to the puppy issue: adopt an adult dog!

Also, if you know you have anger issues, maybe just volunteer at a humane society instead of adopting a pet. You do not want to take the problems that are yours and punish someone else with them. That is not fair. If you know this about yourself, then just be kind, and don't adopt until you are ready. Seek out help from a therapist to be sure, but this is my opinion. Again, I have seen some very bad things happen to pets. (I don't believe in punishing animals to train them; I just reward them for doing things the right way, such as going potty outside, instead of punishing the wrong. An exception to my ADHD, I suppose, is that I have the patience of Job when it comes to animals.)

I have also been the luckiest person in the world to be fully loved by the dogs and cats I have known. I have walked thousands of miles of trails with my dogs in many states; I have driven across country with them; I have shared many hours of play.

There is nothing to make you forget you have ADHD like a dog or cat snuggling into your arms.

I make walking my dogs — early, before I get too distracted — a daily "chore" I have to do, and it is the best and smartest and kindest rule I ever made for myself.

Counselors & Physical Therapy

Sometimes a massage is a great stress reliever. I hardly ever treat myself to one, but when I do, I relax and take the time to just chill, which I never do otherwise. A clean hot tub or a swim in a warm pool (hard to find!) works the same way.

And then there's counseling. I am considering going back to a therapist, but this time one who is an actual expert in ADHD issues, and certainly not one who just nods in agreement or one who pushes drugs, but we'll see. It takes a lot of work to get to a counselor. And ADHDers can be overwhelmed by the layers of difficulties set in our path for what should be a simple phone call and appointment. Will they require me to test again, for example? Will they require me to go through phone interviews with staff (the *receptionist?*) and fill out questionnaires first, then have an "evaluation" appointment to see if I'm even worthy of seeing the actual psychiatrist, as the one office I called tried to do? Don't they understand how absolutely near-to-god-impossible this kind of strategy is for someone with ADHD? But then again, that was just one of the few counseling offices on my health care plan, and close to home. Their mindset seems to be to keep people out instead of let them in.

So, I might have to pay a lot more money and travel 50 miles each way to see an actual specialist in ADHD, but it is worth considering, if I can't find the knowledge and support I need elsewhere. If I need an extra boost. (Especially, if I need someone to help me and my family communicate better, which is my biggest concern.)

But just knowing that there are specialists in ADHD out there, available if I need them, is in some ways a relief of sorts. I don't honestly know if I'll ever be able to make that appointment, but for the purpose of this book, I aim to try, so I can share my experiences with you.

If you're not comfortable with a certain therapist, just go to a different one. No hard feelings. It's your life. It's your money. It's your time. You are hiring them; they are not in control of your life. Remember that.

Oh yes, and don't read the novel *Saving Grace* by Jane Green. It'll scare the crap out of you and you won't want to go to a counselor at all!

(I made the mistake of listening to this novel on CD in the car. It would have been so much better to have the actual physical book; I could have hurriedly read through to the end. So now I just listen to nonfiction audio books while driving. Perhaps this is part of ADHD hyperfocusing, but it is also the unbearable slowness of the reader of the audio book; my mind doesn't work like that. If I'd had the book, I could have finished in two hours – okay, well, maybe six since I'd probably get distracted and do two dozen other things while reading it.)

Where *Not* to Go for Support

You know them. They are the people who bring you down, make you feel bad, use you, take from you.

Leave them behind.

Don't waste your precious life with them.

It's the same with physicians, psychologists or psychiatrists, or other professionals that you hire. They are supposed to be working for you. If you don't feel that they are, then let them go, and don't feel bad.

If you can't decide, just listen to the song "Let It Go":

> *Let it go, let it go*
> *I am one with the wind and sky*
> *Let it go, let it go*
> *You'll never see me cry!*
> *Here I stand*
> *And here I'll stay*
> *Let the storm rage on!*

— Lopez-Anderson and Lopez, "Let It Go"

The reason I feel "Let It Go" is a great theme song for ADHD has to do with what happened while my father was ill with cancer, some 20 years before Disney came out with the movie *Frozen*. The phone was in his game room, where his sick bed was, and I received a call from a former co-worker who rattled on about the terrible things our boss was doing to the company and everyone in it. I got riled up and upset about it, about how I was treated there, even though I had left and moved back to Alaska to help care for my father.

After I hung up, I started to tell my dad about the situation in the office, all wrapped in the anxiety of remembering working there, tediously talking about people he didn't know and never would.

My father, sick with cancer, life being shockingly shortened well before he was of retirement age, just looked at me, pale and quiet, and said softly, "Let it go."

I sat stunned, silenced, for once.

He was right of course.

None of this meant anything, in the scheme of things.

Sometimes, when my ADHD brain goes crazy worrying or focusing on something that troubles me, I try to remember his words, his quiet manner, his soft, gentle way.

"Let it go."

2. My Treatment Approaches #2: Medication

Diary of a Ritalin User

July 31, 2015 – Day 1

Taking a Pill is Not So Easy

So I've had this prescription for 10-mg Ritalin (actually generic Methylin) sitting in my cupboard for four years. I guess I've been afraid to try it.

Today I tried it. Yes, it's expired, but oh well. We know how that works. It would require another appointment with a doctor 50 miles away, explaining (which I couldn't do) why I didn't try it before, wasting more money.

It says,

> *"TAKE 1 TAB AM EARLY PM AND INCREASE BY ½*
> *TWICE DAILY EVERY 3-4 DAYS IF*
> *TOLERATED/NEEDED UPTO [sic] MAX 2 TAB 2XDAY."*

Sure, as if that's not confusing to the ADHD brain. I'm thinking that whole mess means two pills a day, one in the morning, one in the evening (is it early morning or early evening? Where is the period, comma, or semicolon to guide me?). I'll start with mid morning and early evening. That same simple sentence suggests I might need ½ pill more (what time? When? With the other two?) after 3 or 4 days "if tolerated" (what does that mean?) or "needed" (how do I determine that?) up to max 2 tab 2xday (so four pills a day? When? Why? How? By what time ... ? How long? Do I take ½ pill extra for 4 days, then 3 pills for another 4 days, and then 3½ for 4 more days, and 4 pills for the rest of my life? What the fudge?)

Telephone Calls, Son, & First Pill Tears

Anyway, this morning is one of those days where I've convinced myself to do some of the "nasty" chores, which for me includes returning or making phone calls. I'm not someone who enjoys being on the phone, especially when it involves waiting or listening or punching numbers. Yuck.

So I take a pill. And wait.

I don't have to wait long. A warmth shovels its way through my frontal lobes. It scares me.

Crap. It's not a good feeling, like Xanax, but something deep and serious.

So this is the power of Ritalin, I think. Can I still think? Yes I can. In the meantime, the healthcare.gov person has finally gotten on the phone. While waiting six boring minutes, I managed to put away the dishes, scrub the sink, open and microwave a can of soup, fill up the dog water bucket, move the laundry to the dryer, fill the water bottles, and about half a dozen other tasks. This is not because of the pill. This is what I do while on hold on a phone call; I don't sit still well. I think that's a good thing about me, honestly.

So a few minutes later, I'm done with the call (they have to call me back in 5 to 10 days), and I'm back at my computer and eating my soup while paying bills online, and my son comes in my office.

I'm always happy to see him. Even if he doesn't know it.

"I'm taking ADHD medicine," I tell him, "just in case I seem different or weird to you."

"Why are you doing that?" he says.

"Because," and then I start to feel emotional and cornered and hateful of the feeling in the brain which is not my brain now that it is on drugs, "you and your dad say I interrupt too much, and – " I stop, not knowing what to say next. For once.

"You don't have to do that. We don't mean that," he says, shocked a little.

I start to cry a little. I don't know why. Must be the damn Ritalin. "I'm not myself," I mutter, angrily, resentful, glad his dad isn't here, because I'd really blame him. Thoroughly. Light into him in fury.

"I'm sorry," I say to my son. "I just want to try the medication for a few days to see if it helps. It's not your fault."

He backs out of the room. I wonder what's going through his mind. But by then I'm off to a dozen other tasks, and I accomplish quite a bit, giving myself 30 minutes to do them, taking 45, and then off for a dog walk.

My Dog Has ADHD

So, today was supposed to be the Big Day When Mom Achieves One of Her Goals for the Summer: Climbing the Butte.

I was only going to take the puppies, because the older dogs – Blue and Chewie – are having troubles with tough hikes these days, and Miza, well, he's Miza.

I manage to get the puppies downstairs and the door closed with the older three dogs upstairs, but my son lags behind.

When he opens the door, Miza, of course, comes bursting down in all his raging barking growling mess of madness.

Fudge.

SO wants to know why we have three dogs going with us. What he really means, of course, is "Why is Miza going?"

Now, Miza has gone everywhere with us for the last 6 years (feels like 20 or 30), but he is the worst dog in the world to travel with. Especially if he doesn't have "his" seat ... the front passenger seat. He bounces back and forth, barking and growing furiously, terrorizing the puppies, jumping on me and scratching my legs with his 65 pounds of horror.

Miza is my least-favorite dog I've ever had. (Actually, I can't say I've ever really known a dog I didn't *like* before him. And I do love him. I just don't *like* certain parts of his personality.)

I knew within 10 minutes of taking him out of the pound that he was trouble, but I certainly wasn't taking him back.

He is an anxious, crazed, mouthy mess. He never settles down. He won't stop complaining.

He is me, in a dog. (How did I not realize that till now?)

Brat. Miza, you're a brat for being a mirror to my ADHD face; in fact, you are almost 100% the "H" (hyperactive) in ADHD.

I thought he'd settle down once he knew he was our forever dog. "We don't give dogs back," I'd say, scratching his silly black ears. "You can relax now." But he's crazed, in the brain, somewhere. Still, he's grateful, and he tries hard, but it's just not in him to relax.

I've even tried getting medication for him, brain drugs, like I am now trying for myself, but some kind of doggie downer in his case, "just so I can drive to Anchorage and back some 80 miles without him breaking my eardrums," I beg the vet. (The vet prescribed Prozac for him.)

The drugs made Miza furious. He seemed to know he was not himself, and he became even angrier while trying to stay connected to what he knew.

It was kind of fascinating, actually, watching him fight the drugs which were supposed to mellow him into a Zen state of calmness. He was always victorious, coming out of the epic battle between Miza and Miza's-brain-on-drugs more cantankerous than ever. So, drug fail. I tried about three or four times and gave up (which is probably what I'll do with Ritalin).

There is no doubt Miza loves us, completely, fully, and protectively, by the way. It's just that he's a little hard to be around sometimes. A lot hard.

In fact, today, after about 30 minutes of Miza's barking and SO's complaining, I told SO, "Just turn around." And he did. It's the first time in all these years we actually gave up before arriving at our destination with Miza. Maybe we're too old. Maybe it's my medication. But I couldn't stand one more minute of his furious leaping, jumping, whining, crying, barking, growling mess of a dog throwing himself around the van, terrorizing everyone, jumping on my lap, barking in my son's ears…making us all miserable.

I wonder if this is what my ADHD makes others feel like?

I guess climbing the Butte will have to wait for another day. ADHD dog ruins it!

August 1, 2015 – Day 2

The Second Pill & Heart-Pounding Terror … but the Goldfish Are Happy!

Last night I was afraid to take the second pill, but I finally did. My brain didn't feel warm and strange, and I didn't cry, like after I took the first pill, but my heart raced like crazy. I was, honestly, scared, terrified of dying from medication that is supposed to make me better.

I looked up the side effects (after I took it, of course, idiot) of Ritalin, and one possible side effect is weight loss. "I'll take it!" I think, even though after the first pill this morning the front of my brain felt odd – not me. I'm so pathetic!

Of course, for some stupid reason – Ritalin? – yesterday I ate the worst thing I've eaten since I started my weight loss journey almost seven months ago: a large order of onion rings from Dairy Queen.

Why did I lose control eating? That's not like me, not like the new me anyway. It has to be the Ritalin! Dang. I suppose I'm going to be one of those rare people who gains instead of loses weight on the stuff. I found one site (ehealthme.com) that says only 2.98% of people *gained* weight on

Ritalin, but interestingly, **19.05%** of people **age 50-59** (like me) gained weight. I check other sites (such as talkaboutsleep.com) for personal experiences, and some say their appetites were actually stimulated by Ritalin.

But I survived. I took ½ a Xanax to calm my heart down, quit chewing nicotine gum, and finally, eventually, slowly, found sleep. But before I fell asleep, I started a giant project of cleaning and moving the aquarium, which ended up requiring the entire family's involvement before it was done. It took about 2 hours. I'm thinking that might have been Ritalin-driven, since I've been "thinking" I "should" do that for at least two weeks, but I chose last night. However, another inspiration was the Fitbit I got in the mail yesterday; I still had 2,000 steps to go to achieve my 10,000 steps goal, so I met it by aquarium cleaning.

Today is a new day. I walked the dogs and ate first, then I took a Ritalin. I waited because I was scared. But my brain feels fine. I even had a fun drive (with SO driving and without me bitching!) with the family to a little train ride (literally, "little trains" that you sit on and ride around the woods on tiny tracks), and I felt absolutely completely happy for those 20 minutes or so. Then we stopped by an audio store so we could sit in the dark room on the giant couches and watch the giant TV. I actually felt content while sitting still in both situations! Maybe Ritalin will help me. And SO and I got all the way to town and back without arguing. Miracle!

I still have some nasty paperwork to do, which I am avoiding, so I don't think the pills have helped there yet. I just want to go to bed and watch a movie instead. Typical for me.

And I am hungry. Why? I thought Ritalin was supposed to take away hunger. Rats. Was hoping for an "easy" way to lose these last 15 pounds (yes, I lowered my weight loss goal to 145 since I'm now in the 150s; I am a brave old woman!).

Impatience & Worrying

A couple hours after I took the second Ritalin of Day 2, I find myself impatient with watching *Fat, Sick & Nearly Dead* on Netflix. The documentary makes me worry about my son's nutritional habits (as he now eats cheese pizza, which he does about every day, and drinks soda, which he only does about once a month). I come back to the computer to work on one of the tedious tasks that I must do this weekend: typing in all the changes to my address book from the past year to the new year, so I can print it for my new planner, which started today (of course I made zero progress on this).

But instead I start reading up on essential tremor, which my son has recently been diagnosed with. Which leads me to reading about multiple sclerosis (MS), which is what I'm terrified he has, but the neurologist said he "probably does not." In fact, he was more insistent than that.

Still, I will never forget last fall when, at 14 years old, my son came to me and said his plans to be a heart surgeon were "over."

"Why?" I asked. I wasn't taking that goal so seriously anyway. Who knows for sure what they'll be doing for their career at 14? (Hmmm. I guess I did. I knew I wanted to be a writer. Even if teaching, document design, running nonprofits, technical editing, and being a musician – as well as a dozen other "menial" jobs during high school and college – took precedence most of my adult life.)

"Because my hands shake."

"Your hands shake?" I said doubtfully. I hadn't noticed it, so it couldn't be true.

He held them up. They shook pretty vigorously, actually.

"Hmmm," I said, pretending I wasn't worried. But, of course, I was.

Scared – to – death.

Then school and work and puppies and life got in the way, so I didn't get him in to see a doctor. It was probably the ADHD in me that got distracted. Even from this.

Then one day he passed out. Right in front of me. For just a few seconds. Just standing in the living room talking.

"Do you notice our son's hands shake?" I asked SO that night.

"Oh yes, I've mentioned it to you several times."

"No you didn't."

"Yes I did. Over several years."

Dang. The curse of the ADHDer. Maybe he did mention it. Maybe they both did. And it got lost in the chaotic gravel pit of my brain. I just wasn't listening, per usual, although I thought I was. "Inattentiveness": one of the signs of ADHD.

By the time I got my son to a specialist, it had happened again, although he denies it. I heard a crash. He had fallen in the living room again, but this time I wasn't there to see it. "I just fell," he said later, but right after he said he'd "passed out."

Blood tests and an EKG were performed and the specialist was seen, but "essential tremor" became the diagnosis without the tests I wanted: a CAT scan or MRI or something! The doctor asked him to balance on one foot and asked if his legs trembled. "No," he said. I wanted to scream, "This kid is scared of doctors!" (even though he wants to be one). "Don't trust his answers; just test him!"

A lifetime ahead of shaking, no real known or understood reason why. And no, he probably can't be a heart surgeon. It might make "some" patients "uncomfortable." (I know I would be!)

That diagnosis was sad, but it should be a relief, too. Essential tremor is not going to kill him. It's not, other than denying him only one possible career choice (the one he happened to choose), going to affect his life.

But do I take relief in that? Sit back and praise Jesus?

Not tonight.

Instead, I am frantically searching MS websites, trying to call my brother the doctor, then my sisters. I wanted to ask whether they think my boy has MS, and oh my god what do I do? I'm panicking in my head, but if anyone looked at me, typing away, they'd see nothing wrong. It's…all…in…here. Inside my brain. Fortunately, no one answers the phone.

I've always been told that Alaska and Oregon – the two states I spent almost my entire life – are the states with the highest per-capita occurrence of MS. (I can't confirm that online.) Vitamin D deficiency is the concern. Also, if your mother gave birth to you in the spring (like I did), you are at higher risk for MS (probably because the winter-long fetus didn't get enough Vitamin D). Smoking increases the risk for MS; of course, my son doesn't smoke, but his mother did, until this year. Crap. It's all my fault. Of course it is. I'm the mother. The flawed, stupid, crazed mother.

I love him so much.

I have also known – closely – four people with MS, including two I grew up with who died fairly young from it, one by the time he was 30; the other, Tom, a few years ago, although he suffered from it for years, finally in a wheelchair. The last time he drove was to see my son in the hospital just after he was born. My boy grew up visiting Tom. A few days after we went to see him a few years ago, Tom was hospitalized, then died.

MS scares me. My son's tremors scare me.

I sit here, obsessing about it, alone, except for my journal.

Visiting Friends & Is It Me or Is it Ritalin?

Later: Anyway, I suppose it's my ADHD mind that drives me to research scary scenarios, or maybe it's just being a mother, or maybe it's the Ritalin – Day 2. But in the middle of my research, husband-wife friends stopped by and we went for a walk in the wilderness with our dogs (well, not all of mine), and I felt like I was listening better and not so interruptive. But by the time they left, I felt interruptive, flighty in the brain – same old me, and in addition to that I had the racing heart and an awful headache and a tremendous hunger – all new to me, so due to Ritalin. I don't feel good, let alone better.

But let me give it a few more days.

My brilliant but odd brain figures out shortly after blaming the Ritalin that no, I actually often feel this clash of feelings when these same friends visit. What starts out as a relaxing, incredible walk through the wilderness turns into hours at the couch discussing stressful topics, such as children who don't excel enough or are having medical issues, politics, books we've each read but no one else has, our medical issues, various things we agree on but don't quite mesh on, so it becomes an increasingly difficult conversation, and plus it's five hours past when I usually climb in bed with the dogs.

I love my friends, I'm glad they visit, but the personalities of B and I have been at odds since the first moments I met her, when she told me to *slow down, speak slower, I don't understand you*, etc. etc. and on and on during a meeting for a nonprofit I was leading.

"She's a slow talker … crap!" I must have thought.

Over the years, we've adjusted to each other. I try with all my will to slow down my rat-a-tat mouth trying to keep up with my rat-a-tat brain (the one good thing for me about visiting New York City, for I tend to panic in big cities, was how fast people talked – God, I loved that), and she tries not to publically humiliate me anymore. We have come to care about each other. We have in common multiple injuries, a similar age group, and being old parents of a single child. Oh yes, and we have pets.

And our brains don't work "normally." Somehow.

We disagree on drugs; I keep insisting she toss her pain pills by presenting myself as the model of great Throw It In the Septic Tank Before

You're an Addict behavior, and I have before that expressed my horror over her going to a psychiatrist who "only" prescribed drugs after one meeting with you (you brought your test results with you). She convinced me to go see him as well, years ago (I'm sure my fast, interrupting brain/mouth combo drives her to the wall as much as her slow one does me), and he is the doctor who prescribed Ritalin to me.

As she's leaving, I ask her, "Do you remember Dr. F-?"

After a few seconds, they both do.

I briefly say, "I finally tried the pills he prescribed from for ADHD years ago, the last 2 days, and I feel wrong. In my brain. Not myself."

Her answer: "I finally tossed the Adderall and something else he prescribed me and my daughter."

Wow.

"I decided I didn't have ADHD," she said.

Well, duh, I thought.

"I would never called you ADHD," I said, but they were going out the door then, so I couldn't explain. How could she be? She moved slowly through life and thought. Her brained moved as carefully through conversations as her steps through the woods. She listened well and thought things through. Even after our first meeting, hundreds of times after, she has told me to "slow down" my words, and "stop talking so I have time to process."

She is the friggin' opposite of ADHD! Same doctor though. How odd is that? I start to doubt his medicine; not the diagnosis, since he didn't do it. Maybe Ritalin might not be right for me, but shouldn't he have followed it up to see? (Actually, I was probably supposed to schedule a follow-up visit, and it got lost in my thousand things to do. Or his office called, and I wrote it down somewhere and lost it, as I tend to do.)

August 2, 2015 – Day 3

Dog Walking & Talking

Took my morning Ritalin earlier today, before the dog walk.

For the first time, I left the ADHD dog, Miza, at home, as he was ensconced in my son's room and didn't know we were leaving.

"Shhh," I told SO. "Let's get out of here before Miza knows!"

It was such a quiet, peaceful walk without him. But I felt guilty, more than once, tried to call my son, who ignored my call because I always ask him to do something, so then I sent him a message on Skype to walk Miza a "little." (He says he did.)

The walk was good. SO and I didn't argue once, which is highly unusual. Maybe it's because Miza wasn't there, creating barking chaos.

But perhaps it was probably because I am on Ritalin. Plus I kept us busy worrying, bringing SO into my worrying mess, and then my sister, who finally called back, about the possibility of my son having MS. We feel helpless since the neurologist said it's not, so we'll wait and see. I guess. Or should we insist on more tests? See that damn ADHD brain? Can't decide. Going back and forth and numerous other directions, always considering options, never doing any of them.

Come on, Ritalin, work your magic, and make me a better mother!

Pill Confusion

I don't like drugs. I dumped almost all of mine, except for some reason I hung onto the Ritalin, and I know why I hung onto the Xanax (so I could sleep).

There is one pill I do take very day, every morning, or I'm supposed to. Some days, like today, I don't remember if I took it. It's Synthroid, for my thyroid, which has a big ole benign tumor on it and has for at least 12 years. Other pills I try to remember to take daily, and hardly ever do, are supplements: a multivitamin, vitamin B12 (since I'm vegan), calcium, vitamin D (Alaskan), vitamin C (never remember; just bought some because I heard it helps former smokers heal), flaxseed oil and turmeric (for the fibromyalgia pain), Probiotics (because I read they help the stomach), and fiber tablets (not so much an issue now that I'm vegan).

I've organized these supplements dozens of times into little pill boxes, but then I get confused and not sure what's in there and whether I really need it and whether I took it that day, so I end up dumping them in the garbage.

So today I searched online for a pill record. I found a free AARP Word version at assets.aarp.org, which looks like this:

	What I'm taking	Form (pill, injection, liquid, patch, etc.)	Dosage	How Much and When	Use (regularly or occasionally)	Start/Stop Dates (1/5/05 – 3/5/05) (1/5/05 – ongoing)	Notes, Directions, Reasons for Use
	* Be sure to include ALL prescription drugs over-the-counter drugs, vitamins, and herbal supplements						
1							
2							
3							
4							
5							
6							
7							
8							
9							

That's just a list of medications, not what I want, but it might be handy for some, so I'm including it. So instead I make my own, which is in a new tab in Excel, so I can record it daily: Easy peasy!

Prescription Meds Log

Date	Name of Medication	AM Dose	PM Dose	Amt.	Notes
8/2	Ritalin	X		10 mg	started 6/31
8/2	Synthoid	?		1 mg	take a.m. before eating
8/2	Baby Aspirin				optional; supposed to be for heart health
8/2					
8/2					
8/2					
8/2					
8/2					
8/2					
8/2					
8/2					

Supplements Log

Date	Name of Supplement	Took Today	Amt.	Notes
8/2	Multivitamin			
8/2	Vitamin D			
8/2	Calcium			not sure if I need this
8/2	Magnesum			
8/2	Vitamin B12			
8/2	Vitamin C			optional
8/2	Probiotics			optional
8/2	Fiber			optional
8/2	Turmeric			for fibromyalgia
8/2	Flaxseed Oil			for fibromyalgia
8/2				

Next I uploaded this form to Dropbox and printed it for my notebook, so I can share it with any physicians I see. Here's why this is important to me: One time, it took me months to get into a surgeon who might be able to help me with my neck injury, which caused the kind of pain that makes you want to scream all day long. I'd been suffering from it for seven years. His staff sent me a ream of paperwork to fill out, and I got it all done before the appointment except the list of medications. I only had the Synthroid, plus a couple pain pills that I tried not to use to keep my mind sharp for work, but instead of filling it out, I put the pills in my pocket and drove the 40 miles to his office.

When I walked in – early, for once, because this was a life-and-death appointment as far as I was concerned, the receptionist asked, "Do you have your paperwork?"

"Yes," I said proudly, grabbing the gargantuan pile out of my purse and handing it to her. "Except for the list of medications; I have them here."

"Then you'll have to reschedule," she said abruptly.

"What? No!" I sputtered, filling out the information on the form from my pocketed bottles as I spoke, handing it to her.

"That's our rule," she scowled, furious.

"It's done; it's filled out, and I'm on time!" I complained.

She made me sit there for hours – years it felt like to me – in punishment before allowing me to see the doctor.

I was so upset I was going to tell him what the hell I thought about his staff, but then he looked up from my chart, looked kindly into my eyes, and said, "I think I can help you."

I cried a little, right there, all hatred for his stupid ass receptionist and her stupid ass co-workers who made me sit there all day gone, because it was the first time in seven years where I had hope that the screaming pain from the pinched nerve might finally be gone.

(But still, I let the memory of some bully receptionist trying to punish me for not filling out the medications list in advance overshadow all the good that came from seeing Dr. K, who ended up saving my neck and my life.)

In any case, all the organizing I did today was simply an ADHD ploy to avoid the organization I *actually* need to do: the boring, horrible, hated, annual updating of my address book, so I can print it and put it in my planner. Today, I have to do this. I must switch to my new year's planner, which started yesterday. But, typical for me, I am getting everything else done *but* the necessary project at hand. (The only exception to this is work I am paid to do – I always jump right on that, leaving everything else behind, hyperfocusing and unable to do anything else until it's finished.)

Last Night's Eating Fiasco

I woke up this morning to a disaster of cocoa all over my kitchen counters, sink, and stove. I remembered, barely, what I did.

I made a giant bowl of oatmeal, dumped in a bunch of cocoa powder (and clearly missed), stirred in some peanut butter and Stevia (for sweetness), and ate it all.

Was it the Ritalin? Was it the Ritalin plus the Xanax? I don't know, but not good. Yesterday was already my worst eating day since starting my diet, and now to see this mess and know what went into my body, probably around 11 p.m. I try not to eat after 7:00.

Jeez. What was that about Ritalin being used as a weight-loss medication?

Anyway, the good news is I got a lot of exercise in yesterday thanks to the Fitbit: 17,028 steps – the most in one day since last August, when I got the pedometer app on my phone. I know this Fitbit is going to be life-changing, especially because people are challenging me right now, and I feel like getting up and taking another dog walk just to pass them!

Plus, the Fitbit told me that last night my sleep sucked, even with the Xanax. I wonder if the Ritalin had any effect on it? I suffer from terrible insomnia, but I thought the Xanax knocks me deep into dreamland. But there's what the Fitbit said: I only actually "slept" 3 hours, 40 minutes. It took me 1 hour and 13 minutes to fall asleep. Seven times I was fully awake (eating oatmeal?). Seventeen times I was "restless." So my total hours awake or restless (4 hours, 20 minutes) were more than my sleep time. Even though I was in bed about 10 hours. Bummer.

Anyway, I'm going to try to take another dog walk or two, but first I'm going to do my stupid planner address book update. Now.

Later: Done. Done for a whole year with that task. Whew.

Tonight's Dosage

I'm not taking tonight's Ritalin. It is 4:40 p.m., and I just don't want the heart racing panic feeling like I'm gonna die. Nor the headache. Plus I want to see if the Fitbit shows better sleep tonight without it.

Sure, I am feeling tired, like I usually do in the afternoon, and if I take the Ritalin, I might be inspired to jump up and accomplish a dozen little tasks. But I haven't I accomplished enough today? I worked on my books; finished my planner; took two dog walks; made lunch, dinner, and smoothies; drove my son's friend home; got gas; made my 10,000 steps; showered (big deal for me); created Excel and Word charts for medication; and read. I do need to somehow find enough energy to go to puppy training class tonight (I usually never schedule anything at night because I'm so exhausted by this time, but I'll just have to make do). Ready for bed, but can't go there yet.

August 3, 2015 – Day 4

Last Night without a Ritalin

We had a puppy class last night, so my son took Harper Lee to her "school" while I played and walked with Kip outside for an hour. Thanks to doing that and my Fitbit, I made 15,178 steps yesterday, well over my 10,000 goal.

I also felt and slept better without the Ritalin. I think I'll just stick to one a day in the morning for now.

Morning Pill

Took my morning pill, then my sister Ellen, the hoarder, called. I tried hard not to criticize or interrupt her (successful at the first; failed at the second). I talked about her ADHD a bit. She was uncomfortable talking about it, but I tried to be gentle and understanding with my new-found knowledge, also slipping in what I read about how having less stuff actually makes it easier on someone with ADHD because they have less to distract them.

"I know if I have a lot of papers," I said, "I start to do something, then I see another pile and shift to that, and then I don't get done what I originally intended."

She spoke up: "Yes, I do that. Like with my craft room, which used to be S's [her daughter's] room, I start to go through things but then I see other things, and I go to that instead."

"Exactly." I think it's the first time I've talked to her about her hoarding without making her feel bad. I could do much better, though. I got irritated with her when I brought up how I like to get rid of stuff and it makes me feel better, and then she started criticizing me for things I got rid of that were mom's or dad's (she's very specific, remembering a certain book I used to have, for example), and I started to get defensive and angry. Then I breathed, and said, "Well, for example, I had that beautiful photograph made into a picture that dad took of the whalers going out at sunrise in Barrow. It was gorgeous."

"Oh yes, I loved that picture," she said. Of course she remembered it, because she remembers every little thing that anyone ever had and wants it.

"Well, I loved the quality of it too, but it always made me think of whale hunting, which made me sad. So I gave it to Randy [our little brother]."

"You did?" She was amazed.

"Yes, and it makes him happy, and it makes me happy that he has it. And it's still in the family." I added that because it would make Ellen happy.

We got off the phone without hanging up on each other, so that's good. (And, per my usual pacing and doing things while on the phone, I got my dishes done and my smoothies made while talking to her.)

Half an Hour of ADHD Madness after a Dog Walk

Next, I took a dog walk. While on the dog walk, I realized my beautifully organized Excel chart of medicine is missing something essential: my dog Chewie's medicine. I remind myself to give it to her when I get home. I send myself an email (which hasn't come through; I don't know why; just thought of that).

So then I head toward the bedroom to get Chewie's medicine, but remember I'm thirsty so I go to the fridge to get water, which reminds me I should take a vitamin so I go to the bathroom, which reminds me I should give Chewie her medicine so I leave without taking my vitamin, which reminds me I should go update my Excel chart with pet medication, which reminds me I didn't add *Garcinia cambogia* to my supplements chart (supposed to help with hunger), which leads me to the computer where I answered several emails, checked my friends' Fitbit progress, checked Facebook, gave an estimate for a report to format, looked up a cost code for a client, checked my phone, and I am now working on this book instead. In between all that I threw the ball for Kip down the stairs, outside, where I see SO had started digging up weeds before the walk, but then I see Miza down the hall looking at me, so I know he's going to race up barking at Kip till he drops the ball, so I walk down the hall to put him in my son's room, where I remind my son he's late at his one weekly chore of cleaning up dog doo, then I go back to throw the ball for Kip, and then I see SO hasn't gone back to finish his weeding, so I go down to the lawn to throw Kip's ball while finishing SO's weeding for him, thinking, he's going to be happy, but he's going to redo it because I'm going too fast and missing some of the roots, but this is only the second time in 10 years I've done anything remotely related to gardening, which, like cooking, I have no patience for.

So just now I turned to the Excel monitor (I have four monitors, remember) to fix it and reprint it. But then I got a phone call, so per my usual method of handling phone calls, I paced the house, going to get

Chewie's pill, putting it in a pill pocket, going downstairs looking for Chewie, telling SO I finished his weeding, coming back upstairs, looking outside and telling my son he missed one, finding Chewie, giving her the pill, finishing the call, going back to my office, finally finishing the Excel sheet, which I printed, which required more paper (fortunately, I reorganized so I have a drawer with blank paper right near the printer now), and here it is at last! Going to go tape the printed copy to the inside of my bathroom cabinet:

| Medications & Supplements Log | | | | | | | | | | | | | | | |
Name of Medication	Amt.	Notes	8/2	8/3	8/4	8/5	8/6	8/7	8/8	8/9	8/10	8/11	8/12	8/13
MEDICATIONS														
Ritalin (Methylin)	10 mg	started 7/31/15 for ADHD; expired pills	1	1										
Synthoid	1 mg	take a.m. before eating	?	1										
Baby Aspirin		optional; supposed to be for heart health	0	0										
Xanax	1 mg	for sleeping	1											
SUPPLEMENTS														
Multivitamin			1											
Vitamin D			1											
Calcium		not sure if I need this	2											
Magnesum			0											
Vitamin B12			0											
Vitamin C		optional	0											
Probiotics		optional	0											
Fiber		optional	2											
Turmeric		for fibromyalgia	1											
Flaxseed Oil		for fibromyalgia	1											
Garcinia cambogia		for hunger	0											
NRTs														
Nicotrol Inhaler	10 mg (4 mg)		2											
Nicotine Gum	4 mg		4											
PET MEDICATION														
Chewie's Thyroid Pill			2	1										
Miza's Calm Medicine			0											
Blue's Pain Pill			0											
Miza's Pain Pill			0											
Worming Medicine	gave 7/25/15	every 3 months for dogs; every month for cat	0											

Wow, that worked awesome! As I took my supplements, I marked them off on the chart pasted in my bathroom. Then I made notes on it and came back to the Excel chart and added columns for Dose and Calories. I also added a Miscellaneous row (hair regrowth drops), and next I'm making one for my son.

You might ask, is it the Ritalin that allowed you to be so productive and awesome? And I would say, "No, I'm productive and awesome all the time!" Plus I'm still distracted and doing other things and still surrounded by (and avoiding) piles of paperwork and numerous to do lists. But the fact that I got my medications log done and printed and put up, and the fact that I got Chewie's pill in her before noon, are both victories, so perhaps it is helping.

August 4, 2015 – Day 5

I feel like I've given Ritalin a good college try to little avail. Even though I dropped down to only a morning pill, I find the heart racing is troubling. Today I actually took ½ a Xanax to slow down the frightening beating heart.

Am I less interruptive? No, I don't think so. Am I less critical of my son? No. I'm still a Negative Nellie. A Nagging Nancy. Am I more productive? No, I don't think so. I'm still surrounded by paperwork that I don't want to do. I still haven't created my new to do list or looked at my old ones.

It hasn't been a miracle worker for me.

Perhaps it's the wrong medication. Perhaps it's because it's expired (but I definitely feel it affecting me in the brain and heart, so I doubt that is it).

I have been very productive today, but that is because I (happily) got two big projects. I immediately did them, dropping everything else, except the dog walk, which I forced myself to do. But there is nothing different about me there. Anytime I get paying jobs, I jump right into them, hyperfocusing, letting go of everything else.

So no, I can't credit Ritalin with that.

And I am hungry. Very hungry. I fight it, though. I have worked too hard to lose this weight, and I only have 5 pounds left to lose to reach my healthwage.com goal, which means I'll win $1,324 (minus the $450 I paid in). So in the past week, I've lost another pound. Typical for me during this journey. Ritalin didn't help or hurt.

How about increased energy? I'd say no. Yesterday I was in bed by 6:00, exhausted from sleeping so poorly the last few nights. I didn't get up till 9:00 a.m. I slept fitfully. This, again, is pretty typical for me, although usually the Xanax wipes me right into dreamland. Even though I changed the Ritalin to once a day, in the morning, I think it still hurts, not helps, my sleep.

August 5, 2015 – Day 6

So this morning I use my handy-dandy medication/supplements list in the bathroom cupboard. It is a tremendous help. I remember to give Chewie her thyroid pill, and I take mine as well. I remember to put the minoxidil drops on my head for my thinning hair. Great chart!

But then I look at the Ritalin. Do I wanna? Should I give it a full week try, at least? I close the cupboard door, not ready yet.

I have to research this Ritalin a bit more before I swallow one more.

But then, just now, I went and took one. I will go for 7 days, I decide. What can it do, kill me? Maybe.

I did, actually, accomplish something last night that I've wanted to do for at least five years but couldn't. I got Dragon Naturally Speaking to work on my computer (thanks to my son's help). Then I went through the giant piles of "to do list" notes scattered around my computer, and spoke them into the computer, watching them show up nicely on the screen. Then, it turns out I did it wrong, and they all disappeared. I Googled what happened, and a lot of people were upset about the same thing happening to them. I looked in the garbage can full of to-do lists, and sadly, I pulled them out, and I started over, this time using the program in Microsoft Word. I did them and saved it. Task completed. Yay! Do I credit Ritalin with that? Or Ritalin plus ½ a Xanax? I don't know, but I'm just happy it's done.

Later:

Okay, within an hour after I took my little Ritalin pill, I felt incredibly awful: headache, heart pounding and racing, grumpy, near tears, klutzy (spilled my coffee all over the place in front of my son's entire high school class at registration), and short-tempered.

If this is supposed to help my relationship with my son, it is definitely not working.

I hate this feeling so much! I feel ready to dump the Ritalin right in the toilet.

(I did, however, manage to fill out my calendar, although I had absolutely no patience for sitting and waiting at my son's school, so I left while he registered. I don't see any improvement in the organization sphere. My desk looks worse than ever.)

Nicotine & ADHD & Ritalin

I noticed my ADHD seemed to get much worse since I quit smoking three months ago (wow, good for me!). It is therefore part of my theory that nicotine (smoking) is a self-medicating treatment for ADHD. Perhaps from the dopamine rush to the head, like sugar does.

I have been getting through being a nonsmoker by continuing to use nicotine replacement therapies (NRTs) such as nicotine gum and the inhaler (not e-cigarettes; I don't see the point of quitting smoking to "smoke"). But the Ritalin has had a positive effect on my use of NRTs, as in, I have to actually see them to remember to chew on a gum, for example. I don't crave them like I did before. I don't feel an anxious desire for them (maybe because I'm so anxious already from the Ritalin).

Taste Buds & Energy

Another thing is the Ritalin gives me an odd tinny taste to my mouse sometimes, but when I do chew the cinnamon or fruit-flavored nicotine gum, it is such a shockingly delicious flavor, much different than before. Which makes me want them even if I don't desire them....oh well.

About four hours after I take the Ritalin, my heart calms down a little, so perhaps I could get by on half a pill.

As far as energy goes, I haven't noticed any increase. In fact, the last two days, without SO to prod me, I haven't made it my entire dog walk around. I wanted to think it wasn't really my fault, but my dog Chewie needing rest, but really it's my general laziness, I think. Is it Ritalin's fault? I doubt it. I am just noting it for those of you who wanted a play-by-play of my trial (because that's all it's gonna be!) experiment using Ritalin.

The Last Day on Ritalin

So I've decided that today is the last day I am going to try Ritalin. I was going to give it one more day, trying just half a pill instead of one (and remember, the prescription was to start with two a day and increase to four; I think I'd keel over if I did that!). But I can't bear one more day of this drug.

August 6, 2015 – Day 7 (No Ritalin)

Wow, it feels nice to be myself again, quite a bit calmer, my heart not pounding out of my chest, no tears, and no Super Anxiety. Here's the deal: I don't think Ritalin should be prescribed to people who are already anxious worriers. Or insomniacs. Just my opinion. And supported by Drugs.com: "You should not use Ritalin if you have glaucoma, tics or Tourette's syndrome, or severe anxiety, tension, or agitation."

Summary of My Trial

So, I am not a fan of Ritalin. I didn't like the way it made me feel; it didn't help my relationships; it didn't cure my disorganization, insomnia, or lack of energy. In fact, I didn't see one benefit for me personally.

Does that mean it won't work for you? Of course not. I just wanted to try a little and see since I had a prescription for it.

I've talked to a relative who is on Adderall. She seems as scattered, disorganized, messy, and hoarding as always.

But that's her, and it might be that a different medication could help my ADHD. Or that trying Ritalin longer might help. Or that getting an unexpired version would help. Or that not using the generic would help.

But really, I know this about me: I don't like taking drugs.

I like my brain. I like my brilliance, curiously, creativity, and talents.

I don't want to change those.

What I do want to control is my impulsivity in relationships: interrupting, speaking out of term, saying inappropriate things, feeling overwhelmingly nervous in social situations. I also want to control my worrying and anxiety.

Those are things I can treat in ways that don't involve drugs such as self-help books, meditation or music, counseling, and self-reflection. Maybe nutritional approaches will help as well. And especially, journaling, as I'm doing here, is an excellent treatment. It helps one do the "self-reflection" just mentioned, as well as keep specific focus on the task at hand, which is, in this case, handling my ADHD. And I love journaling because it lets me share my solutions – and failures – with an audience who understands my "problem."

So I am most happy to be done with my little "drug trial." I think the real reason I even tried those pills was because I saw how much worse my ADHD got after quitting sugar and smoking, and I realized there's a brain chemical issue going on that I was self-medicating.

Well, my new life for the last eight months has been about getting healthy, and I've decided that ADHD medication is not the way to go for me.

I will explore other ways.

Thank you for reading along on my little experiment. Now to go flush some Ritalin down the toilet. Yay!

I'm so happy a drug was *not* my "cure."

At least I got my pill charts made out of this fiasco. Now I can go cross Ritalin off all my perfectly designed and printed lists!

Side Effects of ADHD Medications

Many of the books I've read encouraged the use of ADHD medication to improve one's life. In fact, it seems to be the most common recommendation for "treating" ADHD symptoms in most online articles and books (however, many of them are written by psychiatrists and some studies are possibly sponsored by drug companies; some sites also have advertisements for ADHD medications).

Certainly, this is a decision you and your doctor (psychiatrist?) need to make. Such medications can work wonders on people, they say; be life-changing, they encourage.

Perhaps, if I wasn't 55 years old; hadn't invented numerous strategies to help me be a highly functioning ADHDer, at least regarding work and organization; and if I didn't work at home, I might try other medications in order to seem like a "normal" person to others.

But I'm pursuing other methods for now.

One thing I did want to mention is to be sure to look up side effects of any medications and consider them. In general, according to *Healthline*, ADHD drugs can cause sleep problems, mood swings, appetite reduction, heart problems, and even suicidal thoughts or actions (Story and Goldman).

Rethinking Medication

I've been reading *Driven to Distraction* and *Delivered from Distraction*, books about ADHD by Hallowell and Ratey, which are definitely pro-ADHD medications. The most convincing argument they make for ADHD medication is a metaphor: that it is like giving a near-sighted person glasses so they can see clearly. In the same way, medication can help one think clearly.

I'm certain that stimulant medications aren't right for me, but there are certainly plenty of other options worth considering. I will disclose (in case you don't realize it already) that I don't like taking drugs; I am seeking alternative solutions. I did conduct my "little Ritalin" experiment for this book, but I saw no positive changes in that (admittedly short) time. In any case, I'm not willing to drug-shop or continue trying other medications unless my other Treatment Approaches do not work. However, as the authors write, "about 85 percent of adults will benefit from one of the several medications that are used for ADD." (*Driven*).

Later: I recently learned a child I know and love is on ADHD medication. She and one of her brothers have ADHD, and the medication helped them become "good little students." In his case, I think it was a benefit. In her case, I think it took away her spirit, creativity, and uniqueness.

I didn't know she was on ADHD medication until yesterday, but I knew, about three years ago, that she suddenly changed, didn't seem herself, was quieted and still. She seemed depressed to me. Everyone said, "Oh, she's just growing up."

Maybe.

Or maybe it's the medication.

The other child, her brother, grew up, graduated, turned years of bad grades around and went to graduate school. He is old enough now to make his own decisions about the medication, and he says he only takes it when he really needs to focus, as for an exam.

I just don't know....

3.   My Treatment Approaches #3: Improving My Outlook

Fixing My Crappy ADHD Mood

Maybe the most important thing of all, more important than reading my to do lists or organizing my bathroom cupboards, is changing the stupid ADHD outlook that ruins every day for not only myself, but others close to me.

Like many ADHDers, I have had bouts of depression, anxiety, worry, self-doubt, self-loathing, and a general feeling of *blah*. On top of it all, I have the classic obsessive thinking, finding it difficult to let go of an always-negative thought. As Beth Main explains it:

> *Our minds are always on, often running laps around the same track....*
> *What you resist persists. The more you try to ignore these thoughts, the more*
> *persistent they become.*

One of the solutions for this obsessive thinking tendency? Take a hike! But sometimes that is when my negative thoughts, as shown in the next journal entry, is the absolute worse for me. The negativity seems to loop and build. Of course, this is because of what is happening to where I hike.

Attitude Diary – Obsessive Thinking

So, I just had a beautiful early-morning walk on my favorite hiking trails ever. Only one other car was in the parking lot when I pulled in about 7:30 a.m., hitting it early before the Saturday crowds come along.

I do, after all, have five dogs. This is a serious problem when you want them to run free, wear themselves out, not have to hold them on leashes through 4 miles of trails, but instead have them gallop around and to you, happily telling you about everything they smell and see through the wags of their tails and the happy lolls of their tongues.

So, it is best to go when no one else is there. Plus, I like the quiet time of nature hikes, especially since it seems to calm my brain a bit, as long as no other human being is with me. Today, I left SO behind (as I used to always do before the puppies started showing a bad side with strange dogs a few months ago), and set out on a gorgeous walk with my mutts, all five spinning in glorious happiness around me. The temperature was perfect, about 60, the woods are still green, with the nights not yet freezing the leaves to yellow and orange, then quickly dropping them, which will start any day now. The ravens and seagulls provided the soundtrack.

But then there were those other sounds. Even at 7:30 in the morning. On a Saturday.

The sounds that drive me mad. That have ruined my walk, every day, all day, from 7 a.m. to 7 p.m., all summer long.

The sounds of heavy equipment destroying Trail 12.

I seethe with anger, resentment, misery. I can't focus on the gorgeous trees and feel of the earth beneath my feet. I roll over and over in my mind 13 years of letters, calls, and complaints I've sent to everyone, media interviews I've done, even going and speaking before the parks commission. I feel like my brain is going to explode at that one. The whole public comment invitation was a lie ... the first trail had already been destroyed before the meeting even took place.

"Stop yourself!" I think. "You are ruining another walk with this obsessing over the negative." I know now, through my research, that this is a typical problem for ADHDers. I try to say a mantra, humming "Oooooom." (Probably an affirmation would have been better, repeated over and over, as in, "I am happy and at peace with the world." A lie, but even lies can be distracting, right?) I feel silly and ridiculous, but it seems to confuse my mind away from the equipment noises for a moment. Then I tell my brain to think of something positive, so I start admiring the beautiful leaves and tiny flowers around me, which draws my eyes to the trees, which draws my brain to the sound of trees being toppled by the monstrous excavators the next hill over. I want to scream, but I don't. Maybe I should have.

I am crying now. The dogs are concerned, looking at me. I pet them, comfort them. I wish someone could comfort me. I wish I was Bill Gates, and I'd walk into the government building and hand them a million dollars or however many millions it took, and I'd own these trails, and deem them safe forever. I'd make the excavators back away, stop, forever silenced. I'd make the landfill….ah hell. My mind is jumbled as there is no solution. And I don't want to be Bill Gates; I just want to be friends with Bill Gates or some other super rich benefactor so he saves these trails.

My jumbled, crying, frantic brain. Ah, I feel sorry for myself, but more for the bears, moose, ravens, eagles, songbirds, squirrels, wolverines, porcupines, and hikers and their dogs and horses who make these trails home. I feel sorry for my son, who has grown up on these trails, first in a stroller, now, at last, just as tall as his mother. My poor brain walks through year after year of my son's life on these trails, starting with him in my belly as I hiked them, not even aware yet that he was growing inside me. In first grade he drew this at school, and it is one of my greatest treasures. It tells the story of his childhood, hikes on these trails with mom (who is simply an arrow to the left of the picture) and the dogs:

Then, my thoughts turn to the dogs, all of them, years of them. I see Buddy pausing one day, exhausted only 10 minutes in, telling me something is very wrong with him. He turns around to go home, his walks on the trails forever over. I see Bailey, SO's dog, overheating on Alaska's one hot day ever, the only day I got completely lost in the trails (trying to find the pond, but taking the wrong trail by mistake), and she refused to lie down and stay still so I could run back the way we came, too far too far, and then she heat stroked and died. I see the late-fall night hike where Schatzy refused to walk on the open trails, instead staying in the woods hidden. I knew it meant there was a bear following us. I see the puppies, just this year, running out of the trails ahead of me into the parking lot, right into an elderly lady and her even-older dog, and when I came up, the puppies were barking at the dog, Kip diving in and hitting it with his nose, and I suddenly knew I had a very serious problem I needed to train out of them (and so I have been working hard to do so ever since). But most of all, I see 16 years of incredibly happy dogs, exploring the trails with me, day after glorious day. It was the hour in my day that kept me sane and healthy. That is, until about 3 years ago, when the walks became torturous for me, listening to the sounds of the trails going down, realizing there was no hope anymore.

Sometimes, I feel like each tree knocked down is another part of my very soul and body being destroyed, as if I'm bleeding into the now-bare dirt and gravel where once the forest stood. I am dying, like Buddy, from the inside, only it is not my eocinophils attacking my organs as happened to him, but it is the corruption and lies of a government that can't stop itself from tearing nature to nothingness. It is a world I don't fit into. It makes me want to lie down and die, right there on the trails, like Bailey did, hot and furious, making myself part of them before they are entirely gone.

My very being is one with these trails. I am weary of loving trails and then seeing them ruined. In Oregon, it was both the BLM and privately owned lands leased for logging. In Washington, it was hundreds of acres turned into more ticky-tacky subdivisions. But this all started when I was a child in Anchorage, a city which boomed almost overnight after oil was discovered on the North Slope, and every special place I played in became another house, another street.

"I want to live where it's dying," I've said to SO at least 1,000 times. "Some place where nature is taking back instead of civilization moving in."

"So you're moving to Detroit?" has asked, snidely, the last time.

I'm too old to watch another beautiful forest be destroyed. This one is so completely wrong since the trails are already there. They are well-used and well-loved, but it seems that I am the only one who fights for them, and I'm too drained to continue. I've had my hopes lifted then smashed a dozen times. I have no fight left.

But still, I obsess, cry, and complain and let the thoughts ruin my walks.

Last year, I started walking elsewhere, other trails, other places. That helped my mental state a lot. But now, with five dogs, I am limited on where I can go. I must stick to the trails closest to the landfill, closest to the noises and equipment of destruction, because few people dare to go there but me.

I don't know how to stop letting these thoughts ruin my life, but I must find a way. It is killing me. I come home bitter, angry, unhappy, instead of refreshed and joyous.

> *Gotta get off, gonna get Out of this merry-go-round*
> *Gotta get off, gonna get Need to get on where I'm bound*
> *When did I get, where did I Why am I lost as a lamb*
> *When will I know, where will I How will I learn who I am*
> — *Andre G. Previn & Dory Previn, "(Theme From) Valley of the Dolls"*

Solving Obsessive Thinking Diary

Instant solution: I'm leaving again, taking the two puppies and SO down to the river trails. I'm hoping no one will be there at the banks and I can let them run and chase balls freely without worrying about the puppies (or people) causing me trouble. I think listening to the river and watching my puppies play will free my brain of the anxiety from hearing the excavators take down my beloved trees and trail.

Later: It worked; it was fun, and nice. We actually did run into a guy and his dog. Fortunately, the puppies were still leashed at that point, but even more miraculously, they didn't react, wagged their tails, didn't bark, didn't try to attack. Life is good, suddenly. And later, I'll take the old dogs on other trails, far away from the noise.

But Worrying Can Lead to Solutions...

It's nice to think of not worrying and being happy. But sometimes that doesn't solve anything.

And one thing I like to do is solve problems. Yes, I ruminate on them too much. But then, once in a while, I take action.

Clearly, another way I "solve" my ADHD obsessive thinking is to go with the thought that is troubling me. I journal about it. If that's not enough, then maybe I write complaint letters, and if it still troubles me, and it's important enough, I create a website or Facebook page about it.

Sometimes, like when it's really important, such as the killing of healthy, adoptable pets at animal controls just because of overbreeding, I do something that makes a real difference. I start a spay program, for example. I volunteer for a humane society. I feel like my sadness and worrying are small prices to pay compared to the suffering the dogs and cats go through, and the lives cut short. I might pay a price, but it's a tiny one. I have seen things, bad things, piles of bodies of pets who were killed just because there are too many. I have shed many tears for them, and then I stopped crying and got busy solving.

In other words, we can find ways to turn our chronic worrying into some sort of attempt at a solution.

We ADHDers can change the world.

Or at least we can try.

Worry Busting

Chronic worrying is not necessarily a symptom of ADHD, but it can be part of it (per Hallowell and Ratey, *Driven*), or can be a separate "anxiety disorder" per Healthline ("Relationship") that is often "comorbid" with ADHD. Oh good, I have another disorder. Nice! Per Healthline, ADHD symptoms "primarily involve issues with focus and concentration, rather than nervousness and fear." But right in Hallowell and Ratey's excellent "Suggested Diagnostic Criteria for ADHD in Adults," which I have all 20 of, is this:

> *13. Tendency to worry needlessly, endlessly; tendency to scan the horizon looking for something to worry about, alternating with inattention to or disregard for actual dangers. Worry becomes what attention turns into when it isn't focused on some task.*

Whatever and whoever is right, clearly I worry too much for this short precious life. I need to find more ways to enjoy it, to face my fears, to conquer my anxieties. Denise Mann of WebMD ("9 Steps") provides these "worry-busting steps":

1.   Write down your worries.

2. Analyze your list to see what items are productive (you can do something about it right now) and unproductive (these are "what ifs" that you can't do anything about; there is no solution; an example is worrying whether you'll get cancer).

3. Embrace the uncertainty. This one is confusing to me. It sounds nice to "embrace uncertainty" but what the heck does it mean? Accept "your own limitations" or the fact that there is "a degree of uncertainty" regarding your unproductive worries. Accept that you don't know what the future holds; yes, it might be bad, but it might not be. "Uncertainty is really neutral," so accept that you "don't have to worry anymore." Instead, let go, and focus "on the things that you can control, enjoy, or appreciate."

4. Bore yourself with calm. For this, WebMD suggests taking a worry (or fear) and just repeating it over and over until it becomes dull to you and goes away. "Say it enough and it will lose its power." Hmm. I don't know about that, but it's worth a try. Sounds awful, actually. My worst fear I don't even want to say, but it involves the possibility of a certain loved one dying. It scares me so bad I can't even think of it, let alone repeat it into a mirror. Egad!

5. Make yourself uncomfortable. This is another suggestion that sounds awful to me. Maybe some of these won't work for ADHDers: "Worriers feel that they can't tolerate discomfort, but if you practice discomfort, you will accomplish a lot more." What? I don't even know what they mean! Their example is if you are terrified of public speaking or parties, force yourself to go to them. Okay, I guess I actually have an example from my own life. The first time I gave a public flute performance, as a college student, at the museum, my hands shook so much from my terror that I couldn't play well at all. It was a disaster. My flute was shaking, so I couldn't blow into it correctly. I sweated horribly. What did I do? I signed up for every single museum performance that year. Did I ever love it or enjoy it? Not really. But I never shook again. So I get it. Yes I do.

6. Stop the clock. Worriers tend to fret that if they don't do something right away, something terrible might happen, but the suggestion here seems to be to consider whether that is true. Is it really urgent? I'm not sure this one is helpful to ADHDers; I think

we tend to procrastinate and delay too much already. Maybe worrying is what helps us get things done. However, I suppose it depends on the task. I like the idea of taking deep breaths, playing gentle music, and releasing the anxiety first, then: "Ask yourself, 'What can I do in the present moment to make my life more pleasant or meaningful?'" In my case, that usually involves chocolate, but whatever works!

7. Remember that it's never as bad as you think it will be. "Anxiety or worry is all about anticipation. The 'what ifs' are always way worse than how you feel when something actually happens. Worriers are actually good at handling real problems."

8. Cry out loud. By letting out your emotions, they advise, you are not worrying.

9. Talk about it. Talk therapy can help you get "to the root of your problem." Figure out what is causing your anxiety, dig deep, and go to the roots to make "it go away." Hmm. I guess I worry most about losing someone I love. This has been shattering to me. I don't love many, but I love deeply. I have barely survived some of those deaths. Losing the ones I have cared about has been devastating, whether its my parents, my dogs, or best friend. Most of my worries are about those I love. I am terrified of losing them. Would my life be over if I lost my son (the thought I could not speak above)? Yes, I think it would. I can't imagine surviving that. Or why I would even want to. (No pressure, son.)

Hallowell offers additional tips on ADDitude's website, including educating yourself, taking action about what you're worrying about, visiting people or getting out in nature, seeing a counselor, using medications, changing "the physical dynamics of your brain" (by exercising, listening to music, deep breathing, meditating, praying, sleeping, writing a letter, making a list, or making love), and creating a plan to "address your worry by evaluating the situation and formulating a response." He also suggests that you "trump negatives with positives" in this way:

> *Talk to yourself in a positive way. Most worriers talk to themselves in half-phrases of imagined doom. Telling yourself, "I know I can complete this project as soon as I sit down" is more effective than saying, "I never seem to be able to finish anything!" If you start thinking negatively, do something to distract yourself, such as whistling or singing.*

Tips for Stopping Obsessive Thinking

Obsessing about negative thoughts is not unusual for ADHDers, and it's probably my least-favorite aspect of this "disorder." The solutions:

Journal – put them down in writing and "give them a home" away from your brain.

Focus on some busy task – This could be a video game, a puzzle (I personally like Sudoku and crosswords), a craft, a TV show, Words with Friends…whatever appeals to you to get off the obsessive thought.

Change your thinking about the topic – "Write down the exact opposite of your concern and visualize it," advises Beth Main. So if you think your partner is having an affair, write down that "She's at the mall, shopping for my birthday gift," she says, "then play out that scene in your mind." Or in my case, "The construction work I hear is actually trail improvements; these trails will be protected forever after they are done." (They aren't trail improvements, but a nice fantasy thought, anyway!)

Repeat a mantra – of course, this didn't work for me very well on the trails today, but I should have pushed a little harder. I needed a "short, comforting phrase" (Main) instead of "Oooooom." Examples Main gives for the woman thinking her husband is cheating on her: *I am a prize. He is worthy of my trust.* Here are some of mine and some I found online that might be useful; all you really need is one:

> *I am happy.*
>
> *Life is good and sweet.*
>
> *Nature heals me.*
>
> *I am one with nature now.*
>
> *I am in a good place.*
>
> *Challenges help me grow.*
>
> *I can choose a positive frame of mind. (Or, stronger: I am staying positive.)*
>
> *I can create inner peace.*
>
> *This too shall pass.*
>
> *Today I choose joy.*
>
> *I can stay calm under pressure. (or how about: I am calm?)*

The point is, Main writes, "there's no room for ruminations if you're focused on your mantra."

ADHD Humor

Here's my favorite part of surfing the Web: finding humorous things about having ADHD.

My son started it, actually. As I learn more and then explain to my family what is going on in me – and I'm beginning to suspect, him – my family is nicer to me. One way I see this is how my son shares what he's found with me. Two of my favorite videos he showed me are on YouTube:

- "Sh*t no adult with ADHD says" by TotallyADD.com
- "How to Know If you Have ADHD" by Nigahiga

Things someone with ADHD would never say, per "Sh*t no adult with ADHD says," include the following ones that I completely related to and made me laugh out loud:

- *To make a long story short…*
- *Finished, wow, everything's done on my list.*
- *Hey, sorry I showed up early; I'll just wait till you're ready.*
- *Enough about me; what about you?*
- *Okay, I made a short to-do list with a manageable amount of stuff on it.*
- *I wish TV had more commercials.*
- *Oh boy, paperwork!*
- *I'm sorry, I'm out of fresh ideas; let's just do it the way everyone else does it.*
- *If I do all my homework now, I'll have the rest of the weekend free.*
- *Let's just read the instructions; it will make things way easier.*
- *I'm ahead of schedule.*
- *I should think about this first.*
- *What a great story; I don't have one to top it, that's for sure.*
- *Caffeine, take or leave it.*
- *Smoking? Take it or leave it.*
- *It's a good thing I remembered my phone, keys, and wallet.*
- *The instant something lands on my desk, I handle it.*
- *You talk; I'll listen.*
- *Feeling pretty calm right now.*
- *I'm just going to finish this before I start anything new.*

- *I'd better give myself plenty of time, in case there's problems along the way.*
- *Ah, finally I can relax.*

Great job, guys! And thanks for the laughs! (And since I'm quoting from your video, I'll plug your website and movie called *ADD & Loving It*). The comments to the YouTube video include lots of great ones too, such as:

- *I've never had 200 tabs open on Chrome at the same time.*
- *I like to finish every book I'm reading before starting a new one.*
- *I did all my holiday shopping early so I don't feel rushed.*

If you're feeling bad about having ADHD, search "ADHD humor," including images, on the Web or Pinterest, when you want to distract yourself (ha!) and feel better. Thank goodness many ADHDers can find fun in our situation!

On another note, Kessler argues that many comedians have ADHD, and suggests, "Perhaps 'class clown,' should be listed as a diagnostic in the DSM V...." The trick, she says, is learning "how and when to turn it off – and when you should." Well, that's certainly been the case with me; I've had people literally laughing till they cried with my inappropriate comments at unexpected times (i.e., formal meetings) more than once. I loved the feeling of having the whole room laughing, but I can't say my quirky sense of humor is always appreciated.

Learning to control the jokes from jumping out of my mouth – that's been a tough one.

But one thing I can focus on is comedians, and it's a way to calm my ADHD brain to watch a good one (preferably several short sketches one after the other, such as in *Last Comic Standing*). If I feel bad, a little Amy Schumer or even clips from the old *Carol Burnett Show* or *The Tonight Show with Johnny Carson* gets me into a happy place.

The point is, as comedian and writer Rick Green suggests, we shouldn't "suffer" with ADHD. Enjoy it a little.

The Good News

There is good news about the ADHD state of mind. The more I educate myself, the better I feel. Truly.

I start to understand that these tendencies to obsess over things, worry about things, hyperfocus on work or thoughts, and even anxiety can be a "normal" part of having ADHD. Especially helpful is knowing that there are techniques to handle the negatives and turn them into positives.

Just educating myself about what "normal" ADHD involves is a huge relief. Knowing you are not alone, that others have gone through similar frustrations and found ways around or out of them, is a glorious feeling.

Instead of despising the part of me that worries, I celebrate the part of me that worried to the point of doing something, so that I have literally saved thousands of pets from being killed in my lifetime through spay/neuter programs and volunteering for humane societies, or that I have personally saved hundreds of farm animals from suffering by going vegetarian the day after I graduated from high school.

Instead of obsessing with worry over my son's future, I instead celebrate the good things we've done together and the wonderful qualities he has.

I will continue to educate myself about how to turn the negatives of ADHD thinking into positives, and life will go on, just a little bit easier and better.

Or maybe a lot better.

4.　My Treatment Approaches #4: Diet and Exercise

I certainly don't claim to be any expert, but I am sharing my approaches and experiences with you in the hopes that you benefit from my experience.

Of course, you should see a physician before making any dietary changes, "yada, yada, yada"! (Do all ADHDers love that quote from *Seinfeld* as much as I do?)

Diet

This year, I have changed my diet completely, turning vegan, and later eventually eliminating almost all sodas and sugar. I lost over 50 pounds in the past 8 months, and it wasn't as hard as I thought it would be, even though I am a woman in her 50s, past menopause, with numerous surgeries and medical issues.

And here's another plus: I feel better. All around. Even mentally.

I think sometimes the reason I have been able to accept certain major changes in my life, such as the slowdown in work coming in, is that I am eating fruits, vegetables, and seeds every day. I am feeding my body good, nutritious foods. I am not killing it with sugar like I did before.

As far as there being an ADHD diet, you'll find plenty of opinions and few facts online. There just hasn't been much for actual formal studies, it seems. But Richard Sogn tells *WebMD* that eating a diet high in protein, low in simple carbohydrates (carbs), with a variety of complex carbs (vegetables and fruits), and more omega-3 fatty acids (fish, Brazil nuts, olive oil, flaxseeds, chia seeds) seems to be good for the brain.

The same article ("ADHD Diets") suggests eliminating artificial colors (especially red and yellow), food additives (aspartame, MSG, nitrites), sugar, and caffeine to help reduce hyperactivity.

Personally, I had to *force* myself to eat fruits and vegetables, as I don't like them, and I don't like cooking. My easy, no-stress solution? Smoothies. I make one every day, with such ingredients as sunflower seeds, vegan chocolate protein powder, a banana, frozen fruit, kale, spinach, carrots, flaxseed, chia seeds, ice, and water. Simple, quick, healthy, filling, delicious.

I've also cut out sugar almost completely, which might be helping my mood.

Or it might be hurting it – something rarely mentioned in the books and articles I have researched.

I personally used to turn to both cigarettes and sugar (chocolate candy, cookies, cakes, ice cream, muffins) to handle stress, anxiety, worry, and anger. In fact, I, perhaps like many women, stuffed my feelings, especially anger and sadness, by overeating.

After I removed as options my ability to turn to cigarettes or candy when I'm upset, the ADHD symptoms definitely got worse.

My solution? Exercise.

Exercise

Exercise is supposed to help with ADHD by increasing dopamine and norepinephrine levels in the brain, decreasing restlessness, and improving cognitive abilities for handling daily tasks and learning (Bailey). I don't know for certain that it does. I have been a person who has spent years recovering from surgeries, where I hardly exercised at all except for easy dog walks, to one who has gone to the gym regularly plus rigorous dog walks. I've never really noticed a difference in my ADHD during those times, but then again, I wasn't *paying attention* enough to know if it is truly a help.

It probably is, let's face it. If you're like me, you dread doing it, but you always feel a little better afterwards (even if it's just, "Whew, glad that's over! Now I can get on with my day!").

In my case, taking the dogs for a walk in the woods is usually a wonderful release of tension, unless I start obsessing in my mind about the trails being ruined or worrying about my puppies acting badly, which I do tend to do. Sigh. But then, back home, I feel a little sore and stiff in a good way, the dogs are exhausted and happy, and I can relax.

If I didn't obsess too much, but let my thoughts go other places, I usually work out several problems while walking. Maybe I email myself a note or add to my to do list on the phone as brilliant ideas or forgotten tasks come to me while I'm in nature.

The last two weeks, I have slowly increased my exercise from about 6,000 steps a day to about 12,000 most days, even up to 24,000! The inspiration? The Fitbit. What a great little tool, especially for someone with

ADHD. I like all the statistics that show up on the iPhone app as it syncs with my Fitbit. It's a way of organizing my health, so to speak.

Fitbit Surge

And I can do these great challenges with friends, earn badges, and have a history of my workouts, sleep, heart rate, and more. I can easily scan the barcode of a food and add it to my daily calorie intake. All in all, this is a little life-saving and life-changing tool, I feel, for someone like me. In the two weeks since I've got it, I've lost another 4.5 pounds, which is amazing since I'm so close to goal.

If you can't afford something like a Fitbit, no worries! There are great free pedometer apps for most smartphones, cheap clip-on pedometers, and various apps to help you record your food or exercise. There are apps such as "Map My Run" to track your exercise using GPS. I just like the Fitbit as it does it all. And I especially like having a watch on my wrist again. It's been years, and let's face it, as an ADHDer, I *need* a watch!

For me, as an ADHDer, the best exercise is one in which I am doing at least two things at once: exercising my dogs and exercising me. Plus I might have many other things going on during such a walk: exploring nature, thinking out work or personal issues, listening to phone messages, listening to music, reading emails, etc. So ADHD of me to turn a little nature walk into a multitasking adventure.

The worse exercise for someone like me? A treadmill. It's torturously boring. I have to have music, my phone, the TV, and a book or magazine just to bear it.

But I definitely feel mentally better if I get a walk in (and even feel happier once the dang treadmill time is done, if I ever get on it). In fact, my stress level increases the longer I delay doing my daily walk; whether that is from my feeling guilty for not walking or the growing anxiety of my dogs I'm not sure. A little of both. I've made walking the dogs a habit, and I try to do it as early in the day as possible, so I can relax and do other things (and go other places) guilt-free.

But no pressure on exercise; just do something simple like a walk every day. As Iliades writes:

> Countless studies show that exercise reduces stress and anxiety. "People with ADHD can literally be vibrating with excess energy – that's why they call it a hyperactivity disorder," says Gersten. "The most effective way to reduce hyperactivity is daily, vigorous exercise." One of the best ways to exercise is to be outdoors walking or jogging in the open air.

Overall, I think I get bored with exercise. If I didn't have dogs, I'd probably not do it. But since I started this chapter with a Jerry Seinfeld reference, I'm going to mention something he does here, which might work great for ADHDers trying to make exercise (or anything) a daily habit. Supposedly, Seinfeld puts a year at a glance calendar on his wall, and then uses a red pen to X out each day he spends an hour writing. Per Marcia:

> After a few crosses, he became motivated to see the calendar fill with red. He didn't want to break the chain of crosses, so he kept writing....
>
> "Don't Break the Chain" is very effective for adults with ADHD because it places emphasis on habits. When you have created a habit, you no longer have to rely on motivation or internal effort to start and keep going on a task. Instead, you just automatically perform the task because it's something you do every day.

Nice, simple, makes sense. The good ole red X and a wall calendar. I think it could work, maybe get me to the gym or the treadmill. Perhaps if I added a reward for each month of red X's?

5.　My Treatment Approaches #5: Counseling

The Last Time I Tried to Get Help ... and Was Told No!

I remember last time I tried to find a therapist, a counselor, someone to pop in to see.

I was in trouble ... big trouble.

I was in full-on anxiety/panic/depressed/near-suicidal meltdown of anguish.

It was last fall, about 10 months ago.

I was turned away, on the phone, by the counseling office ... by the friggin' *receptionists* probably, because my mental breakdown was over *puppies*!

They were nasty to me when I tried to explain it. I said, "I need to see someone now. I'm in trouble. I have money. I'll pay for it in cash if you need!" But no! They wanted me to explain the problem.

I tried to, but I warned them that they wouldn't think it was important, but to me it was a crisis.

"What seems to be the problem, ma'am?"

Don't I hate those words. "Tell me in 200 words or less what your suicidal tendencies are caused by, and I'll tell you if I think you're treatment-worthy!"

Ah shit. How am I supposed to tell them what I am feeling? They'll never understand. I'll just hop into it and hope they get it, even if I am sounding like Edith Bunker in my panic:

> *"Um, I was fostering puppies for animal control, six puppies, first it was supposed to be four but then when I showed up it was six, for 3½ weeks; it was only supposed to be a few days but they wouldn't take them back because ... they were busy with their Halloween decorations, well, anyway, I fell in love with them, and I read to them, and I trained them, and I cleaned up puppy poo, and I lost 13 pounds because they were so much work, and now they are stuck in little cat cages in an isolation room and they haven't spayed and neutered them although they promised it would be done Monday — four days ago! — when I brought them in so I didn't feed them and they are crying and they love me and I*

love them and animal control personnel are being assholes and won't allow me to see them and I just want to see them and tell them it's okay and I feel so bad and guilty I want to die!"

"No."

No no no. I felt like a fool. But my anguish — and that's the best word for it, pure mental pain like a knife in my brain — was real. I couldn't function. I couldn't focus. I couldn't stop crying.

I got my three dogs in the car and started driving the only road that leads out of Alaska — not that I was going to leave my son, but just because I wanted to pretend I could escape and drive forever away and away and away from my house where the puppies learned to trust humans by crawling in my arms and now that trust was destroyed because I had taken them back there to that awful horrible place.

I drove for miles, stunned as I relived the conversation in my frantic ADHD brain, and I still could not believe therapy office personnel would decide this wasn't serious. To me it was. Isn't that what should matter when it comes to counseling?

I finally drove home, the mania now replaced by crippling grief, and so I called a suicide hotline. *They* had to talk to me. I was risking everything by calling them. They could send, I figured, little men in little white coats to drag me away to some mental hospital. So they had to assume I was so desperate for help to risk that!

So admittedly, I didn't start this chapter with a positive attitude toward therapists.

(And P.S. The suicide hotline lady was *awesome*. She helped me line up some strategies, and so I ended up going and filing a complaint, and after that I went home and faxed animal control a request to adopt two of the puppies since I still hadn't been invited to see them, and somehow I ended up with five dogs in my bed and my car and my life and ... Good Lord, was she actually helpful?)

(And P.P.S. ADHDers, I'm sure, often add P.S. to their letters, or at least we did when people wrote letters.)

(P.P.P.S. Because we think of things we wanted to say after we finished talking, so we're never really finished.)

(P.P.P.P.S. I'm done now. I think.)

Finding a Therapist Is Not Easy

To find a therapist, second, I call my insurance company. Because I hate phones, dialing is never the first option for me. Before that, I searched the online site, but it didn't list specialties. Just the same clinics that I tried to get help from last fall, to no avail.

Being ADHD, while I wait for an actual person to get on the line, I read the website and then as soon as I hear, "How can I help you today?" I am plummeting into a completely different topic: "Do you provide free nicotine gum? I'm reading your website and it says you do," to which I end up being transferred all over the place and never do get a clear answer. Finally, I get back to someone who looks up ADHD psychiatrists for me, and it turns out, there are none in Alaska under my health plan.

Go figure.

So I hang up and call the first clinic listed on the website that is not in my small town, but the next one over, as I'm pretty sure I didn't call it during the Great Puppy Meltdown of 2014. The woman who answers puts me on speaker phone, where she and a second woman start telling me their incredibly awful process, which is designed to keep you from seeing an actual psychiatrist for weeks, instead putting you through written pre-assessments and phone assessments and stuff.

They never let me ask my question, which is, "Do you have someone who specialized in ADHD?" Since according to my health insurance company, they don't.

But they have quickly turned the power in this conversation around so that I have none and they have it all. They seem rude and gleeful as they pummel me with their rules.

I finally weakly squeak out that I don't need the pre-assessments; I can bring the results of my testing (note to self: find that), but no, she insists, they have to do their own testing. Of course you do, I think, sadly.

How useless; what a waste of money and time; how awful.

"Thank you; I'll call back Monday," I say, then, add, taking my power back, "if I need you." There. Go. Hang up now. Yes.

Not using that place. I already knew that 5 minutes ago, but they had their spiel, and they wouldn't let me interrupt. What kind of place won't let an ADHDer interrupt? Stupid.

So I go to the Internet to search for ADHD psychiatrists, and I find a nice little list at therapists.psychologytoday.com, which actually includes paragraph descriptions written by the psychiatrists (or their staff). Of course, by now, I'm bored with this and onto a dozen other tasks, so I copy the info into a Word document and make it two columns and readable and save it to print for my giant "to do" pile. All in about 5 minutes. So I have 9 pages to go through of this:

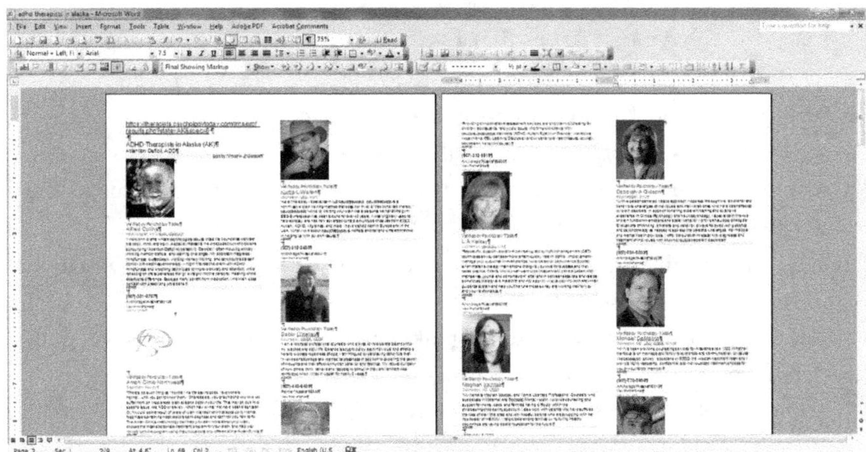

I am awesome with the computer, especially with Microsoft Word. I can do anything with it. And I "hyperfocus" on it, I guess, a term I've learned from studying ADHD. I make it work. I'm the best.

The first one, Alfred Collins, includes:

> *My approach integrates mindfulness, biofeedback, working memory training, and psychophysical self control with depth psychotherapy. I might first teach a client with ADHD mindfulness and breathing techniques to improve anxiety and attention, while reflecting on life experiences that give insight into the personal meaning of the attentional difference.*

I always was scared of terms like "biofeedback," even though some 10 years ago a friend said I should try it. Breathing techniques? Yawn. I am fascinated, mortified, and bored – all at the same time – after reading one therapist's description, and I have about 35 more to read before deciding who is going to help guide me in controlling my ADHD, so I leave it to go walk the dogs – the *five* dogs, by the way, thanks to animal control not letting me visit the puppies and the suicide hotline lady. Five. Dogs.

Another day to go through all the crap I'd have to go through to actually get to sit down and talk to a therapist.

Or maybe never.

Previous Experience with Counselors

I have seen many counselors over the years, even though my mother was dead-set against the idea in general of spilling your guts (brains, really) to a stranger, and paying for the privilege.

But I have had issues that I've gone to counselors for help with.

One is the idiotic tendency I had to date men who weren't worthy of me (or anyone for that matter) and who did things like put a gun to my head, physically abuse me, steal all my money, lie about being married, or be more in love with alcohol than me. (To my credit, I don't make the same mistake twice. Those are five different men I've listed there.)

It certainly seems to be common for ADHDers to attract bad relationships. I don't think we *create* them per se, but maybe we are so insecure and needy and feeling like we don't belong that we grab onto whatever passes by and looks our way.

Which, it turns out, is often a bad choice.

Personally, I never felt "good enough" for a certain kind of man. And then, paradoxically, I felt too good for what I had. I also believed I could "save" and "change" them, kind of like rescuing stray dogs.

Well, stray dogs are grateful. Stray men aren't, turns out.

So yes, I've gone to counselors, pleading for help in getting free, or in fixing a doomed relationship, or to stay my anxiety attacks and tears.

It's been tough, this dating/marrying/cohabitation stuff.

I've also gone to counselors when depressed, such as after my parents died. Or after my dog died. Finally, I went to one while pregnant, as I was terrified of how being a parent was going to change my life. I don't handle change well. (But of course, having a baby turned out to be the best thing ever.)

Generally, my experience with counselors hasn't been all that great. Some just listen and nod and say "Um hmmmm," and some offered medication, and some looked downright bored, and a few actually tried to offer a helpful suggestion or two. None used "tough love," which is definitely what I needed regarding stupid-ass-relationship choices.

What they should have said instead of, "Maybe if you try to listen to him better, he won't be so upset with you," was "Abusers are never going to change; even if he did, you could never trust him; get the hell out of there, and don't look back! Stop feeling sorry for yourself, shut the f--- up, and leave!"

"Bu – But – But I love him!" I would have cried.

"Don't be an idiot. Get the f--- out now."

That's what they should have said. Instead of trying to teach me to "cope" with my situation.

The only cure for a bad relationship is to leave it.

That's my experience, anyway.

Sometimes, you just want someone to listen while you work things out. You can do this for free with friends or family or support groups or chat rooms.

Or can pay a professional to listen.

I've done that a lot, because my friends had enough of my whining, so I didn't have many anymore, and my family didn't know about my bad personal stupid relationship decisions because I was ashamed to tell them.

So I paid a professional.

Eventually, I just had to read up on whatever issue it was myself, work it out in my mind, and leave. Yes, move. Away. Far.

Cures all.

Even – especially – bad relationships.

What the Internet & Books Say about Counseling (the Good Stuff)

So, don't take my word for it. Search the web. One thing I was glad to read is that "traditional, open-ended talk therapies often don't work for people with ADHD" (Griffin). The reason that made me glad is because those are the kinds of therapies I've tried and failed at previously (many times).

So the answer is to find a therapist who actually specializes in ADHD patients, who can help us with our symptoms such as disorganization, forgetfulness, impulsivity, poor communication, and distractibility, as well as the low self-esteem that may be the product of a lifetime of such symptoms. Per Griffin:

> *Most people with ADHD already know what they should be doing. "A guy*
> *with ADHD knows that it's a problem that he's always late on his taxes,"*

Ramsay says. "And he knows the solution, too -- stop procrastinating." What he lacks is the set of skills that will help him get organized. ADHD therapy is typically about learning those skills and finding ways to overcome the impediments that ADHD sets in your path.

"Cognitive behavioral therapy" is often used for ADHDers; the purpose is to challenge "ingrained, negative thoughts" by changing "your responses to them" (Griffin). Another approach is "ADHD coaching," offering practical life-skill tips (such as time management).

Something that does sound useful for me, in particular, is to include the family as part of the therapy, so that my son and my SO understand what ADHD is, how it affects my behavior (such as when I interrupt them or zone out while they are talking), and how we can work together to "fix" it rather than get upset about it.

What If You Can't Afford a Therapist?

If you really can't afford help, and your insurance won't cover it, check for free resources in your area. Or turn to friends for sounding boards. Use self-help books and the Internet to find support groups.

Most of all, believe in the power of **you**. That's what I'm doing. As HelpGuide.org says:

Health professionals can help you manage symptoms of ADD/ADHD, but they can only do so much. You're the one living with the problems, so you're the one who can make the most difference in overcoming them.

This is not to say counseling won't help. I'm just saying to please don't feel hopeless. There is help out there for you, and most of all, there is help *inside* you. You are strong, smart, and capable. You can do this.

I can do this.

We can do this.

Final Thoughts…

I have decided, after researching and even trying, that at this time, I am not pursuing medication or counseling to help me through ADHD issues. Instead, for now, I am turning to books, websites, and online support groups to provide me with the tips and comfort I need.

If it ever becomes unmanageable, though, I know I can go to a specialist for help. Obviously, I am hesitant to do so, based on past experience and current difficulties getting an actual appointment.

However, if it looks like my family would benefit from counseling together, I think this would be the way to go, instead of individual counseling for me. Family is my main concern; personally, I feel that my organizational and work-related skills are strong; where I am weakest is in my worrying, listening, and handling phone calls that require extreme patience (long hold times; having to explain something over and over to different people…the joys of modern times).

The nice part about ADHD is that we can learn to handle many things, such as organizing, ourselves. I'm sure, like me, you've found some solutions that work well for you. As HelpGuide.org says:

> By *taking advantage of self-help techniques, you can become more productive, organized, and in control of your life — and improve your sense of self-worth.*

Of course, if need be, find a coach or counselor. Personally, I am taking comfort in knowing that I am strong (but perhaps not strong enough to handle jumping through the horrendous hoops to get an actual counseling appointment). I am inspired that there are many solutions offered online and in books and by the various online resources such as YouTube videos and support groups.

And Another Final Thought (Coaches)…

Ha! Had to add another "final" thought, right? So ADHD of me!

This thought is about ADHD coaches. They seem to be the "in" thing right now, someone to help you learn to manage your time, your life, your self.

I like the thought of a coach. What I really need is a personal assistant, or an incredibly non-ADHD secretary. And a coach sounds like all that and more.

It would be fun to bring a coach into my life and home for a day or two, and go to town on my files, kitchen, desk, notebooks … just have her (or him) look through everything and assess, evaluate, recommend.

It would be even cooler if she could crawl inside my brain and swim around in there a bit, vacuuming out the stale parts, tightening up the loose screws ("Do you have a screw loose?" my very non-ADHD father used to ask me), and certifying me good to go, another 50 years, have fun!

6.   My Treatment Approaches #6: Deep Breathing, Meditation, Massage, & Toys

Introduction

In this area, I research and try several of the most common treatment approaches online that have to do with the body, whether it's breathing, meditation, massage, or simply busying my hands with fidget toys. I will include you on my journey, of course, glad to provide you with my findings. I am most excited about this part, as they seem like healthy (i.e., nondrug) solutions to ADHD-related stress, in particular.

Deep Breathing

Nothing helped me quit smoking as much as deep breathing. I didn't realize how shallow I breathed until I quit…turns out one of the joys of smoking was the deep, slow inhalation.

So now I try to remember to do that.

Surprisingly, it also seems to help with ADHD symptoms, particularly stress. As Iliades writes:

> *If you feel yourself getting worked up over something, try taking 10 deep, slow breaths. "Regulation of breathing is a proven way of reducing stress," says Gersten. "People with ADHD need to slow their minds down to stop the negative thinking. Otherwise, they can quickly spin out of control." To do this, breathe in slowly through your nose to a count of 10. Feel your abdomen rise as you breathe in, then release each breath slowly as you concentrate only on your breathing.*

My personal opinion is don't worry about breathing through the "nose." Works just fine through the mouth too. And don't worry if you're too bored with it to do it ten times. Whatever you can handle. No stress! Happy breathing!

Meditation

People with ADHD have a hard time relaxing, which includes meditation, hypnosis, yoga, and whatever else New Agey (really old agey?)

stuff is suggested to us. I know I find them all frustrating and silly, like they are wasting my time. I think of other things – more important things – I should be doing. I actually got up and left a college class (not a mediation class!) when a guest speaker started the meditation "stuff." Ugh. Not my personality!

But hey, I'm trying to be a new me, so, deep breaths, here I go, into a brave new world of trying to learn to relax and calm down my ever-busy brain.

Gersten (in Iliades) says that practicing meditation helps the scattered thoughts of ADHDers: "Mindfulness is the practice of learning to be present in the moment, and it's a great way to prevent stress." Iliades points to a study showing a 50% reduction in stress and anxiety for students who meditated, and all you need is 10 to 20 minutes daily.

So how do you mediate? Preston suggests "paying attention to your senses – your body, breathing, and even your voice":

> *Focusing on activities and parts of your body trains you to stay in the moment and helps give you something concrete to refocus on should your mind begin to wander.*

> *You can begin by sitting quietly, closing your eyes and paying attention to your breathing. If you have too much energy to start with something this low-key, you can also meditate while you walk. If you want to try meditating while on the move, just focus on your breathing as you walk or even count your steps – anything that requires your mind to attend to one single activity.*

> *The first few times that you try to meditate, you will probably find your mind frequently wandering. Don't worry. Meditation takes practice. Start out with short sessions, trying to focus for just a few minutes.*

I think teaching my brain to relax and not think a gazillion thoughts will be the most challenging part of my ADHD journey to wellness. Putting one's mind in "quiet reflection and peaceful contemplation" ("Meditation for ADD") might sound like an easy thing to do for most people, but my mind is the opposite of that, all the time. However, it's worth trying, especially since researchers note improvement in stress, anxiety, depression, inattention, and restlessness (all me!) in those who meditate. ADD-treatment.com suggests a way to do "mindful meditation" (Ibid) that seems doable:

> *Close your eyes, clear your mind, and continue to breathe slowly and deeply.*

When distracting thoughts arise, let them gently pass away and refocus your mind on absolutely nothing. Some users find that focusing on the "third eye" in the middle of the forehead gives them an effective meditative focus point.

I was happy to read in the same article that "meditation for ADHD may not be for everyone," so no pressure. Just putting it out there.

But it turns out there are plenty of YouTube videos to guide us on how to meditate, including specifically on adult ADHD ("Meditation Techniques: Adult ADHD & Mindful Meditation"). Just peruse and enjoy!

Yoga

I haven't really tried yoga, and the reason I haven't is because the few attempts I made were much too painful. My body doesn't stretch or bend like "normal" people's due to fibromyalgia; arthritis; spinal stenosis; and neck, shoulder, and knee injuries. Even when I was a child, taking gymnastics lessons and practicing for cheerleader tryouts, my body couldn't bend like others.

But I love the concept of yoga, and it's certainly worth considering for help with ADHD. As Gerslen says:

Yoga and other mind-body exercises are fantastic for ADHD symptoms and stress. People with ADHD spend way too much time inside their heads. Yoga is a way of finding balance between the mind and the body. (qtd. in Iliades)

Healthline suggests that yoga or tai chi may both be useful for treating ADHD symptoms, based on two studies of children (Story and Goldman). It's worth a try, anyway. If your body can take it.

Massage

It's difficult for me, with all my injuries and chronic pain, to find the right masseuse, one who works hard enough but not too hard. It's frustrating to me that so many of them won't listen to me and my needs, but rely only on their training. For example, some are trained to do "deep tissue massage," in which their fingers feel like stabbing knives of pain to me. Sometimes they refuse to believe me. I actually got up and left one massage appointment because she wouldn't stop. (Ten years later, I am still both proud and ashamed of myself for that; I had to physically get up, tell her off, and leave. The guilt is stupid, I know. Mostly, I have suffered silently through those who push too hard and hurt me.)

And then there are those who don't touch you at all, but want you to feel the energy from their fingers hovering over your skin. Are you f-ing kidding me?

But oh, when you can find the right person! The world works for that marvelous hour, and you never want it to end. The suffering lessens, just a little. Your mind goes away.

Well, my mind doesn't. Mostly, I focus on whether they are going to hurt me, or I wish I could put my own CD in and not listen to theirs.

Then there was the last one I tried, a year ago, who actually stuck me on a Wii Fitness while she played with her iPhone. I wanted to scream at her. I did tell her I have a Wii at home and can do this just fine; it was so ridiculous and pathetic. Plus it cost me a wasted $65, which I could have used for much better things, like dog toys! I *should* have screamed at her! Instead, I just never went back.

But, I think of trying again. Just because when it is right, it feels so good.

Toys

After quitting smoking, I found myself buying some busy-hands toys, such as moldable sand, clay, rubber and plastic toys that can be manipulated, etc.

Recently, I ran across an article titled "13 Tips for Buying Gifts for Children with ADHD" (Harding), and I realized that I bought almost every single one of these for my son when he was a toddler, and I actually played them with him, even the board and card games. It was amazing. These were toys I could focus on. Here's what the list included that worked for me (and some still do):

- Play-Doh
- Pin Art
- Fidget toys: Tangle Therapy, Triple Jellyfish Yo-Yo, Breaded Spaghetti Ball. Personally, I like kinetic sand, squeeze or stretchy balls, bendable toys, Water Wigglies, and puffer balls. If you type "fidget toys" on Amazon, you'll see plenty of options!
- Speedy games: Hisss (great card game) and Apples to Apples
- Board games: Candy Land, Connect 4, Chutes and Ladders, and Sorry

- Active Games: Twister
- Large puzzles with not too many pieces
- Constructive construction: Guidecraft's Interlox or Valtech's Magna-Tiles
- Explore the outdoors: Large magnifying glass and Extreme Suction Bug Vacuum (which supposedly doesn't hurt the insects)
- On the Move: Ball Hoppers and Bilibo
- Craft Kits (simple, big pieces; not too many parts was best for this ADHD mom)
- Books: We did a lot of "dot to dot," maze, hangman, and other puzzle-type books (of course, my son wanted to make his own mazes, which involved taping together over a dozen pieces of 8.5 x 11 papers, and they quickly became far too complicated for me). I also enjoyed coloring with him.

The amazing part of this article is that I thought I was buying all these toys for my son, but I was actually buying things I could play *with* him and keep my attention focused.

Many of these toys aren't just for kids, or they don't have to be. Just stop by a creative toys store (or shop online) for items that might help you relax or just keep your hands busy. After quitting smoking, I carried around a baggy of my kinetic play sand in my purse, always ready to fidget with. It was very helpful.

So today, I shopped online for some squeeze balls, etc. that will keep my hands busy while trying to focus on phone calls or actual one-on-one conversations. Win-win. Here are some of the "fidget toys" I ordered:

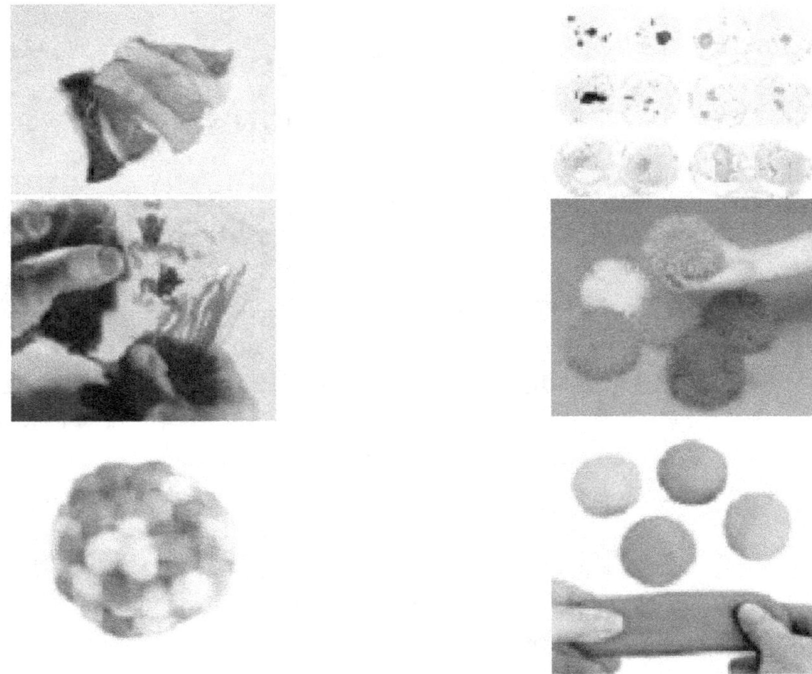

Fidget toys.

Later: I got them, and they are perfect. Nice little things to keep in the pocket or purse for boring times, or even while sitting in meetings, watching TV or a movie, or carrying on a conversation.

Of course, some women I see knitting or crocheting, and I always think that's a similar trick…a way of calming one's brain while listening. But I don't have the patience, the desire, nor the physical capability (due to fibromyalgia) to knit or crochet. Still, it looks like it could be a great solution if you can. In the meantime, I'll just play with my fidget toys!

7.   My Treatment Approaches #7: Journaling

I have turned my life completely around this year through journaling.

I started with a weight-loss journal, writing down everything I ate and drank, as well as my daily exercise (including steps). I also wrote down my feelings and studied nutrition and the reasons I overate. I have completely turned my health around and found my body again.

I decided to try the same approach to quitting smoking, after hundreds of failed quit attempts. I journaled, every day. I researched how to quit, why to quit, benefits of quitting, and successful quitters. I set a quit date, and I did it! Today, it has been four months since I quit cigarettes, and I haven't looked back (okay, maybe once or twice I looked back, but I didn't smoke!). The most I ever made it to before was 21 days, and that was 21 days of misery. Journaling helped me. It gave me a stable, strong point of reference, a friend to turn to, a commitment.

Journaling, it turns out, is a great technique for ADHDers. For me, just having a daily habit of writing thoughts down is part of time management; there is the journaling ("me") time before getting down to work.

Here are some the advantages to writing things down:

- Helps manage our stress.
- Helps control our symptoms, specifically, managing our "scattered" way of thinking.
- Helps us figure out which tasks take priority.
- Gives us a place to "bitch" or rant about our problems, getting what we're obsessing about out on paper and therefore out of our minds (at least that's the idea)
- Offers a place to work with the creative aspects of our nature
- Becomes an easy place to write down to do lists and tasks
- Is a tool to help us focus on issues that are overwhelming us
- Improves our attention span (for some of us, the process of writing helps)
- Provides a place to write down memories, thoughts,

problems, ideas, experiences…before they are "gone."

Personally, I cannot overemphasize the power of writing to help organize ideas and thoughts and turn them into actions. I especially love writing on a computer, where we can put down our various and scattered but brilliant ADHD thoughts, and later go back in to cut and paste and move things around and work things out, so that the very process of rewriting becomes an organizing tool for our minds.

I love journaling most of all.

8.   My Treatment Approaches #8: Managing Distractions

Ways to Fight Distractibility & Boredom

In case you haven't noticed by my descriptions of getting up and going to the kitchen, then doing at least a dozen other things, I tend to get distracted, like most people with ADHD. But I am fortunate that when I have an actual paying project, I hyperfocus, I don't move, and I get it done. (This can also be a problem, as I can work 10 or more hours straight without stopping; I tend to not let go of a project till it is completed.) If you can't focus on one task that you need to do, though, HelpGuide.org suggests prioritizing, breaking large projects into small steps, and using a schedule or timer to stay on task.

Ah, the evil distractions. According to Tartakovsky ("7 Tips…"),

> *Distractibility is a big issue for people with ADHD. They don't have enough activity in the area of the brain that controls attention, said Ari Tuckman…. That means you have a harder time filtering out things you don't need to focus on. "So a kid dropping a pencil in class pulls at [your] attention just as much as the teacher announcing the next test."*

Many things can become distractions, including "sights, sounds, physical sensations, your thoughts and ideas" (Tartakovsky). For me, my mind seems to be thinking of several things at once, almost all the time. Imagine a racetrack with 10 cars on it, only they aren't all together, and they aren't going the same direction or the same speed. Some are stopped; some are actually racing; some are slowly chugging along. It's a mess out there, jumbled together. I try to make sense of it. Each car is a thought.

Maybe I'll ask SO, as I've done a hundred times, "What book are you reading now?"

He looks at me suspiciously, knowing the ropes, but then a little eagerly starts to tell me about his latest tome, maybe something about Andrew Jackson or Johnson or I don't know. I'm already thinking of something else. He's going on and on, but I have heard nothing.

"Do you think the puppies are doing better?" I suddenly ask, and I don't know why he's glaring at me. "I mean, I think they are. They don't seem as fearful of other dogs as before the class."

"Did you hear one word I said?" he demands.

"Of course I did, it's just that I wondered about the puppies, and oh when are you going to the store next? I'm out of bananas!"

He pauses, which drives me crazy.

"Well, are you going tonight, or should I get some tomorrow?" I'm slightly irritated with him now. Why didn't he just answer my question?

He starts to talk, but of course I'm not listening, and I suddenly get up, thinking of how much work I have to do. "Let me know when you're done with the paper," I said.

"I'm done," he says, and I grab it on the way out.

I don't understand why he's always irritated with me.

Ha!

Race cars, just a slew of cars in my brain, all mixed up and none headed for any semblance of a finish line. What a mess!

However, when I focus, boy do I focus! It's called work, and the computer, and no matter what anyone says to me, I don't hear them. I pretend to nod and carry on a conversation, but of course I don't remember what they said. I am focusing on a project, and there's nothing else in my mind at that time.

It's probably why I love working so much. It's the only time my brain calms down and relaxes.

Now, instead of a car wrecking yard, I see a tunnel, long and smooth and perfect, with one simple light far ahead of me.

ADHD experts call that "hyperfocusing." I call it beautiful.

Distractibility and Work

I've been fortunate that generally I have done well at work. But for the last 15 years, I have worked for myself, in my own home, in a perfect ADHD-friendly environment I created, with soft lamp lighting, multiple monitors, a comfortable chair, the keyboard set at the right height, in an office I designed to be a perfect rectangle (my favorite shape) and cozy with books. Plus I have my dogs, which is always comforting to me.

Once I was minus the distractions of overhead bright fluorescent lights, awful cubicles (which I hate more than anything), noises of people visiting with me or others, meetings, etc., I did exceptionally well at work. According to Tartakovsky ("7 Tips…"), "Many adults with ADHD don't realize the degree of their distractibility…. Or they overestimate their ability to return to a task after they're interrupted."

I'm pretty good at this, but I had to take steps to eliminate distractions. For example, I deleted all games from my computer and my iPad. I want them for work only.

"The computer is not *fun* for me," I tried to explain to my son. "It's a tool. If I let it control me, I would be *its* tool."

That's not entirely honest; it is fun. Work is fun, for me. Especially when I have lots of different kinds of projects to work on. The more the merrier, the cliché goes, and it's true for my ADHD brain. As long as it's on the computer, not requiring in-person meetings or phone calls.

In fact, the last job I walked away from required my "presence" in 3 to 4 hours a day of meetings. They actually accommodated me by allowing me to call in, but I found it too tortuous. I could not focus well enough. I quit before they found out. I know myself, and a good listener on the phone I am not!

But why I was telling my son this is because he hyperfocuses on a computer game. "I've been there," I tried to tell him. "After my parents' died, I played Solitaire and Minesweeper for hours and hours and hours, because I couldn't sleep and they sucked my thoughts out of my head and grief from my heart." I even wrote a poem about it:

Games

Solitaire
Minesweeper
Solitaire
Minesweeper
Solitaire Minesweeper
Solitaireminesweeper
solitaireminesweepersolitaireminesweeper
minesweeperminesweeperminesweeper
solitaire …
after you died.
Continuous, days into nights into daybreaks
orderorderorder
icanwinicanwinicanwin
Before you died
I stared at the t.v. screen, never watched, never saw, never heard,

just stared, just remoted, remoted, remoted.
Then it came
as it was supposed to
Father gone
remoted remoted remoted ...
But Mother.
That was not expected.
Alone now,
in the house you raised me in,
not hearing your coughs or snores upstairs anymore.
Solitaire
Minesweeper
Solitaire
Minesweeper
Solitaire minesweeper
minesweeper minesweeper
mindsweeper
mindsleeper
solitaire.

The thing is, an ADHDer, or anyone, for that matter, might decide to check Facebook or look something else up on the Internet, and then – poof – hours are gone by. As a business owner, it would upset me to hire someone who is actually only productive half the time (or less!) that I am paying him for. On the other hand, it would be great to have an ADHD hyperfocusing employee! I'd feel like I was getting twice the work for the same price as a "regular" employee. So…good and bad of ADHD.

In my case, when I've gone back to temporarily help out in an office, perhaps when their editor is on leave, I find the pace much too slow. I feel guilty for getting paid my hourly rate when so much time is wasted, listening to people talk, going to meetings, reading emails, responding to emails, the chatting…. Argh! It drives me crazy! I can't believe people are paid for this!

At my home office, I only charge for the time I am actually reading a report. If I get up for any reason, I stop the clock. That's the way I am, the way I feel most honest and fair. We should be paid only for the time we are actually working.

Working in offices drives me nuts!

Of course, there's the other part of ADHD, the wonderful creative side. This is the part that has been beaten out of us (I hope not literally) since childhood in schools. If a child is looking out a window, is he distracted, or thinking?

"Just a minute. I'm thinking!" my son has said to me so many times in the car, when I rambled on about something. He's staring out the window, and his mind is clicking away. He really is lost in thought. He's trying to work out some idea. He kindly lets me know when he's done, so I can chat away. Poor kid.

Still, I admire this in him; how rare or nonexistent is it to have someone just say, "I'm busy now because I'm *thinking*." But why shouldn't it be perfectly acceptable, and not only that, encouraged? My quiet, thinking time is on my walks; that's why I want to take them alone but rarely can now since I have so many dogs.

Once in a while, I'll get up early, before anyone is on the trails, or I'll take a second or third walk, just taking two at a time, and then I get my quiet, thinking time, alone with nature.

Good for you, son, for reminding me that sometimes we just need to shut up and think.

Finally, consider what you are being distracted by, says Copper (qtd. in Tartakovsky): "Your distractions might reveal the things you're naturally curious about, which you can even leverage." Amazing concept. My thoughts (and written words, you've probably noticed) often turn to my dogs, especially since I rescued the puppies, one of which has fear issues. I am taking more and more classes, and reading books, about dog training, studying "reactive" dogs, which I've never had the "joy" of experiencing before, but now that I know about them, I spend many hours studying how best to help them. It might be that my "distraction" will become a vocation someday.

What To Do

In researching distractibility, I'm glad to see I'm doing many things right.

I have shaped my environment so my office is ADHD friendly ("It's easier to change your environment than it is to change yourself," says

Copper [qtd. In Tartakovsky]). As I said before, I have multiple monitors; no distractions (e.g., noise); lamp and natural lighting; and books, paper, and files easy to grab and all in one neat rectangular-shaped room.

The last couple months, after my perfect office chair broke, I have been distracted at my computer because I'm in incredible pain (back and fibromyalgia). For this reason, I know that I have to make the hour-long drive to get a new chair. Not looking forward to it, but I will do it.

(Next day: Good job. I got up from my painful chair the second I wrote that, grabbed my purse, and headed to Anchorage to get my new chair. Tried them all at two stores, found the one I want, and brought it home.)

Even with my perfectly designed office, I have found that doing "nasty" ole paperwork projects in restaurants works better for me than trying to do them at home. As Tartakovsky says, "If the sound of people talking bothers you, work in a conference room…. If a cluttered desk is distracting, remove some of the disorder or find an empty workspace…." I do my mail and bills elsewhere, and then I mail them immediately. I try to do this at least once a week, usually Friday. (If this is a problem for you, try putting it in your calendar: bills and paperwork Fridays from 10 a.m. to 1:00 p.m, for example.)

I've eliminated games from my electronics. One thing I've left on for social and boredom factor is Facebook, but if it is taking too much of my time, I even delete that from my phone for a while, until I am finished with projects I need to do (this is usually not work-related, but things I dread doing, such as taxes).

Like many with ADHD, I work well under pressure, with set deadlines. For example, today I had two forms to make, which I did first thing this morning, then sent them to the proofreader. In the meantime, I received a report with a Sunday deadline (it's Thursday now). I have scheduled it for five hours this afternoon, and I'll be done and it will be back to the client by tonight. I love deadlines.

Some sites recommend ADHDers set a timer for starting specific tasks or chores, such as 15 minutes, and then maybe a timer for finishing them. It's a way of setting deadlines for yourself. Rayburn tells Tatakovsky:

> *Also, use a timer for checking in with yourself. When it dings, Rayburn said, ask yourself: "Am I doing what I intended to do?"*

There is an easy, free way to do this; just type Google Timer in your browser, and this will pop up:

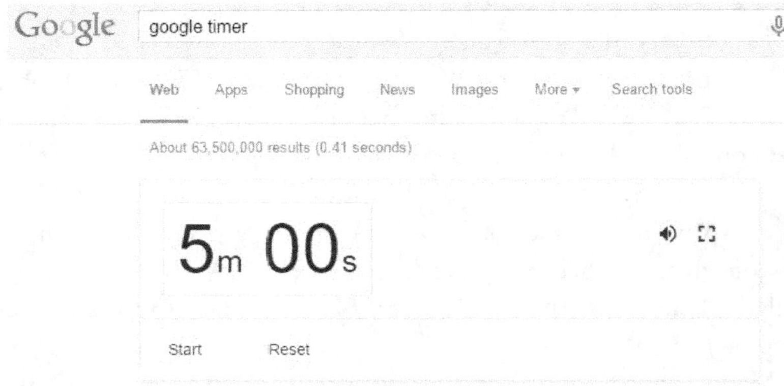

Google Timer

Taking care of my health is something that my ADHD can be both a plus and a minus for. So, since I work at home, I have to schedule in my shower, first thing in the morning, or I get distracted, and I did the same with teeth care and taking vitamins until they became a habit. Otherwise, if I turn on the computer, I might get lost in the work that is coming in.

But ADHD is a positive in that once I have formed a habit, such as exercise, or keeping water bottles with me (and therefore drinking them) at all times, I'm good. I have to walk the dogs in the morning, by 10:00 a.m. This is "not an option." I have made it a part of my daily routine, so I'm good. What is hard is adding an afternoon or evening workout; so far, I have failed at this. But in the past, I have made it a habit, or a requirement (no TV till I treadmill for an hour, for example).

Some people do well with "white noise" or music in the background; I don't when I'm editing or writing; I just want silence. But I've often thought just wearing headphones or ear plugs to drown out the constant cubicle noise when I have to work at an office that's not my own might help me focus. Of course, music helps while doing mundane tasks like cleaning or cooking, but I rarely am organized enough to find a CD and put it in. And certainly for work on such things as forms (requiring patient design work, but not the kind of detailed "thinking" attention editing does) or paperwork, music or "white noise" (in a restaurant, for example) is useful for me. In fact, when I was in college, I'd often go to an airport, mall, or fast food restaurant just to study. I could get completely lost in my textbooks as long as I had the noise and shuffle of other people around me.

Who knows, maybe this was loneliness? It worked, anyway.

Frequent breaks help me; physically, I have to get up and walk around at least once an hour because of the fibromyalgia, but it turns out this is recommended for ADHDers as well, to help them regroup and refocus on their tasks.

Overall, you know what works for you and what doesn't; maybe you just need to sit down and journal it out a bit, make notes, get it straight on paper and therefore in your mind.

Notes on Reading

Reading is my life. It's my "bread and butter." My ability to read well, and to edit well, are what paid for my house and car, for example. When I couldn't focus on technical reports, I got scared, as I've said.

Then I thought back to how I managed my ADHD and did so incredibly well in college compared to high school. It's because I could mark up my books, and boy did I mark them. As I explained before, I learned to write summaries at top of every page. I made notes in the margins.

Even when I read on an iPad or iPhone, I like that I can insert comments or highlight using Kindle.

It turns out, with the editing, I just needed a break. I had been overwhelmed with thousands of reports over the last 20 years, and worked long days and nights, 7 days a week, editing. Anyone would get tired of that.

Now I am rediscovering reading for fun. I still like to read with a pen in hand, if a hard copy, which keeps me focused, ready to write notes, at least with nonfiction. It's a trick that keeps me from being distracted.

9. My Treatment Approaches #9: Organizing Space

Overall, like many adults with ADHD, I have developed many tricks that help me manage my "specialness" over the years. Even though I've been dealt an ADHD hand, I've learned ways to function. Some of these ways have helped me to be incredibly successful, so I'll share my best strategies with you in this section.

Managing ADHD through Organizing "Stuff"

I can't say I ever liked the word "manage." It's dry, dull, and reminds me of cubicles and terrible bosses.

But I'm changing my attitude toward it.

I like the idea of "managing" my ADHD. Per HelpGuide.org:

> *Once you become accustomed to using strategies to help yourself, you may find that managing your symptoms becomes second nature.*

And one great way to do this is through organization.

Organizing is one the ADHDer's most overwhelming tasks, driving us to some sort of inertia or despair, surrounded by piles of things to do that never seem to get done, perhaps just shuffled about, or, in my case, hidden in drawers, cupboards, and file cabinets. I wonder if other ADHDers like to took at the organizing aisles of stores (or posts online) for ideas and containers to properly contain our stuff in, but then we never get around to using them?

Do you have lists, like I do, of things to organize, but then forget to read or ignore your lists, although you always know they are there and feel badly about them?

The main strategy that has worked for me is during my frequent walk-throughs of a room to try to organize or put away something. So half an hour ago when I walked to the kitchen (I have no idea why), I ended up doing these things, not all of them helpful, but most were:

> *Changing clothes, doing laundry, petting the dogs, making tea, doing the dishes, filling the dog water, wiping down the kitchen counters (while bored waiting for the dog water to fill), taking a vitamin, removing the couch blanket to wash, hanging up a bag in my closet, and putting away the toilet paper in my*

bathroom.

About 15 minutes later, I was running a background format check on a document, so I got up again. This time I did the following:

Put a new blanket on the bed, took the clothes out of the dryer and put them in the appropriate rooms, hung a purse up in the closet, put the Goodwill bag back on the dryer (out of site), got dishes from my son's room, started the dishwasher, found my glasses (the original purpose of my "trip" through the house this time), made coffee, washed the glasses, petted two more dogs, poured myself some coffee (even though it wasn't done yet; I was too impatient to wait for it), lit a scented candle, got everything off the dining room counter, and came back to my office at last.

Whew! But I don't feel tired; I feel invigorated. Not only did I get several things done, but I managed to get a lot of exercise in those few minutes! I added another 1,000 steps to my Fitbit. Win!

But wow, I think of how living like that must look like to someone without ADHD. It's exhausting just reading about it. I've always been a little jealous how SO can sit in his chair reading all day, perfectly relaxed; it also upsets me a tad because there's "so much to do"! I actually keep a "to do list" just for SO although I try not to print it for him but once a year. The way we "get along" now (and we definitely haven't always in the past) is that we have a duplex; I leave his stuff alone, and he keeps his stuff out of my space. I can organize and sort away. He can hang onto everything, and I don't have to care.

Breaking huge projects into small steps is recommended by just about every site out there. Following are some of the things I do that have helped me manage my ADHD, long before I knew I had it. (Sources include Helpguide.org and Hallowell and Ratey, but mostly my own personal experience in living with and managing my ADHD for 55 years.)

Create a specific space for things you need daily, such as keys, and always put them there. I recently put a small red basket on the kitchen counter just for this purpose.

Get rid of clutter! Toss, store, box, or donate what you don't need and what distracts you. I put books on bookshelves, clothes in the closet, everything in its designated drawer. I don't like clutter most of all, so I hide what I can, then go back to sort and organize it when I have time or make time for it (often while being on hold on the phone).

In other words, keep things out of site and in drawers – yes, my drawers are messy, but the rest of the house isn't.

Keep extra trash bags in the bottom of all trash containers (and trash containers in every room); go through once a week and grab the trash bags and dump them (and open a new one).

Keep a Goodwill bag handy. Mine is on the dryer, so as I'm going through the house or closet and see something to donate, I put it in there immediately.

Consider a daily walk-through. I walk through the house nightly to clean off desktops, table tops, grab laundry, hang clothes, and start the dishes because I so enjoy waking up to a clean, organized home.

Keep small items in separate containers that look like the picture below (when I was a teenager, I used the fishing tackle box my dad gave me for my makeup). I keep one in my office (tacks, staples, stamps, and other office supplies), one in my bathroom (makeup), and one in my utility room (nuts, screws, and small tools).

Source: colormob5k.com

Store like items in the same place, together. For example, for my pets, I keep the dog food in a container that is sealed and hidden in my cupboard. I feed the dogs twice a day, at about 9 and 5. I keep all the dogs' toys in one drawer, their medicine in one cupboard, and their brushes and extra collars, etc. in another drawer. For my cat, I always empty the litter every Sunday, and she has a similar feeding schedule to the dogs. Dog and cat canned food is stored on one shelf in my kitchen.

This brings up the next point: store like foods together in the cupboard. I also like using plastic containers for some food items.

Use shoe organizers that hang over doors (pictured below) to organize various items. One contains winter hats, gloves, and scarves; two contain electronics plug-ins, chargers, and wires; another contains miscellaneous supplies such as eyeglass cases and dog brushes and other pet supplies:

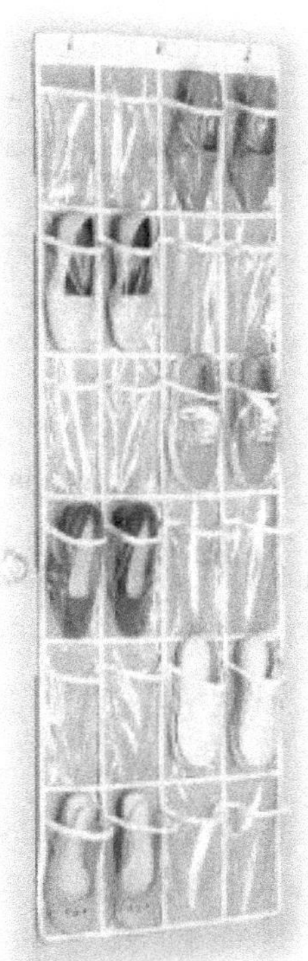

Source: amazon.com (Whitmor Shoe Organizer)

Keep like books together, such as animal books, novels, self-help, writing, and reference. That way you know just where a book is when you need or want it.

Keep CDs and DVDs in organizers; get rid of the containers they came in.

I function best when I keep things sorted and organized; it's a constant battle to do so. For example, I try to keep a separate drawer for socks; and I try to match them up right after I get them out of the dryer. If I don't, I have a chaotic sock drawer, or maybe socks mixed in with other items. I want to be able to quickly find the socks I need, easily, with no stress.

I have learned the same technique helps me in other areas of my life. For example, I need to take water and bear spray on my dog walks through the Alaskan woods, but I hardly ever do. I did pack a backpack with water and bowls recently, since one of my dogs is getting old and having trouble on the walks, so as long as I keep that hanging by her leash, I'll remember it. I also made, in the process of writing this book, a checklist reminder for dog walks (so I don't forget the bear spray, for example!).

I try to keep a pen and a notepad handy at all times (next to my bed, computer, and in my purse), as my mind thinks of "things to do" constantly. Recently, I've started to use the iPhone for this as well; it makes grocery shopping much easier.

Cupboards & Drawers

Slowly, since starting this ADHD journal, I've started organizing my drawers and cupboards, and it has made my life so much simpler. I just do one or two a day, and they are almost done.

Now, for the first time in years, I have socks in one drawer, under things in one, bras in one, stretch pants in one, summer wear (such as swimsuits and shorts) in the last one. That is one organized chest of drawers. I no longer have to paw through the drawers to find what I need.

I have a drawer with just pet items in it, such as toys and brushes. I have a small cupboard that contains their medications, vitamins, and ear drops.

I have a cupboard with canned pet food on the bottom row, soup on the middle, nothing on the top (since I can't reach it).

I have a drawer with plastic lids. I have a drawer just for silverware, and a separate drawer beneath it for larger kitchen cooking utensils.

And so on. Slowly my life gets easier as I know where to go, exactly.

10.   My Treatment Approaches #10: "Smart" Phones

Good Uses of the Cell Phone

The smartphone is my friend in most ways, like these:

- When I'm standing in line, I don't have to be bored and frustrated. I always have something to read or do.

- I can leave the computer and go out for walks with the dogs as long as I have a smartphone. Before, having an online business, I was forced to stay at the computer pretty much all the time, in case I received an order.

- I have my calendar and clock right on screen, in front of me.

- I have handy to do lists and other apps to help with organization and reminders.

- I can speak into the phone and add more "to do" or "buy" items right when I think of them (unless I'm driving, of course), which is great for someone with the scatterbrain syndrome of ADHD.

- I can keep all my essential information handy. For example, I have started taking photos of important documents, such as my dogs' rabies vaccination certificates, and then saving them to a Dropbox file which I can easily access. Sometimes, such as when I lose a phone, or computer, which I've done (the laptop was actually stolen – taken right out of my book bag while I was in line at the cable company, where my distracted bored self was looking at cell phones), my worst fear is that someone will know what they have, because all my passwords and account numbers are in that little cell phone. So far, no one has stolen my identify, so I think I'm good. But I can't tell you how many times it has helped me to have that login information or account number handy.

- Banking: I used to be overwhelmed by bills. I'd let them pile up till I'd finally pick a day to go to a restaurant or bar, and sit for hours paying them all. I also mailed in all my checks for deposit, as I didn't want to try to schedule a trip to the bank into my busy days. Now I just use mobile banking for everything: bill pay, deposits (you just scan the check in by taking a photo of it!). So simple, fast, and nice. Plus, at the end of the year, I have my records all online for taxes! And ADHDers *hate* tax time!

- "Use the cell phone as a tool, not a toy," I tell my son. For example, in school, he could take a picture of the white board with all the assignment due dates written down, and then transfer those dates to his calendar later. I do the same thing; I look for apps to make my life easier. I try to use the phone, not let it use me. Recently, I have downloaded a free app called "Wunderlist" that is so far my favorite for keeping track of things to do on the iPhone, but whatever works for you. One thing for sure, it's fun to try many of them when you're bored.

Not Good Uses of the Cell Phone

However, the smartphone can also be my enemy, as in this:

- When my family is talking, it is tempting to look at the phone while listening. In other words, not listening. This upsets people, and rightly so. Recently, I went to lunch with a friend who spent the entire time texting with her grandson, whom she lives with! Without explanation, I got up and said goodbye. It was so rude of her, so I was rude back. I vowed to never do this to anyone, and I haven't … um, except my own family. Oops! Going to work on that one.

- I tend to always want to be "doing" something, so the smartphone is too easy to use to take videos and pictures of my son, for example, who hates that, instead of actually just focusing on him and what he is doing (soccer, a play). It didn't hit me full force till recently when I saw a photograph of Donald Trump speaking to a packed crowd in Arizona. The photo showed part of the audience. It seemed like all of them, instead of looking at Donald, were looking at their phones that were videotaping Donald. Why? Will we ever watch these videos? Do we need all these photographs? I vow to do better by my son, and my dogs, and not photograph them so much but instead be more present in their lives.

- Meetings are the worse for me. I love having a cell phone to read the news, check Facebook, etc. instead of paying attention at the meeting. I'm not sure if this is a good or bad thing, actually. It would depend on the meeting, I suppose. If it was for work, and I was being paid to be there, I would definitely avoid pulling the phone out. (However, note that the younger generation, especially, sometimes uses the phones for note taking, so don't assume people are "playing" during meetings. They could be working.) I've actually thought about going to church, but the last few times I tried, it went on for hours, and I thought I'd explode from anxiety and boredom. If I could pull out my cell phone, I think I could manage it, but I know that would be considered bad behavior (although not sinful!), so I just don't go.

- Facebook. Me bad. Too much blabbing about things I shouldn't blab about. From boredom and ADHD. Too much honesty. Too much tirading. I'm sure my "friends" grow tired of me. I grow tired of me. And how many pictures of my puppies do they need to see, anyway?

- Games. I deleted Words with Friends. I found it a huge time waster (and of course I was spending hours a night playing it). It was incredibly addictive. I'm not even going to try Candy Crush. These games suck you in and never let you go. I don't play them. I don't want to go there, spending my "middle age" and golden years playing stupid games. I see what Clash of Clans and Minecraft do to my wonderful, smart son. It's a constant battle between us. Life is too short for me to give myself to these games.

11.   My Treatment Approaches #11: Managing Paperwork & Time

I have found tools to function – highly function, I would say – while having ADHD. Maybe ADHD helps us actually do better than most. When it comes to managing time and handling paperwork, we develop systems that work for us. Here are mine; I am hoping that in sharing these techniques, you might find something that works for you. Or you might have better ones yet.

Paperwork System

I wanted to call this chapter "Taking the Paper out of Paperwork" because the Internet, smartphones, and online banking have all helped clear those piles, made things easier, and simplified my life. But there's still paper to be dealt with, so I'll talk about that here.

Design a paperwork system that works for you. I know that if I throw all the paperwork into a book bag and drive somewhere else to do it, leaving books, computers, iPads, and other distractions at home, I can get it done. I do this about once a week. I stopped picking up the mail daily and instead do it on the way to this Big Paperwork Day Project Which I Hate. Then I don't have to think about it other days. Perhaps it would help me to actually schedule such a day into my calendar.

As much as possible, I've gone paperless. It has taken me a long time to trust this system, as I actually like hard copies of bills coming to me, especially since I receive 3,000+ spams a day. But I've started to switch to electronic statements, and I definitely love my bank's Bill Pay and Mobile Deposit features. Nice!

File Cabinets & What Goes In Them

I am very talented at filing.

Sure, if you looked in my file cabinets, you would see chaos. For one thing, I don't have typed labels (my father did), but instead have probably unreadable (to everyone else) sloppily handwritten titles on my folders.

But the main thing is, everything is organized in folders, and the folders are mainly organized into the correct drawers, some even in alphabetical order! For example, I have the following file drawers:

- 2015 Records and Receipts (in alphabetical order for quick filing ease and finding a receipt for a return; titles include Bank, Car, Credit Cards, Home, Insurance, Medical, Pets, Store Receipts, Work)

- Previous Years' Records and Receipts

- Animal Issues (I've been collecting articles since high school on various animal issues; some of the files, entire drawersful, I did manage to toss before my last move, because they were educational, and that information is now available online)

- Published Articles, Stories, Reports, and Books

- Draft Publications (yet to be finalized and published)

- Personal files

- My son (his schoolwork, pictures, and medical records, for example)

- Volunteer Work Records (since I oversee a nonprofit in my spare time, I keep all the paperwork here)

- Photographs (yes, after getting them all scanned last year, I put the original photographs into a file drawer to store them)

I can't imagine anyone on this earth actually enjoys filing, but I appreciate being able to find something when I need it.

I only actual "file" all the new items into the correct Records and Receipts folders about twice a year; until that time, I put all receipts and paid bills in a "To Be Filed" folder.

January is my self-imposed deadline to get everything filed, organized, and done; then I tortuously pull out all the last year's receipt files relevant to taxes, and slowly start typing them into Excel, all in preparation for the accountant to do my taxes. It takes days of misery, but then it's done. Every year I vow to do it differently, keep up the Excel file as receipts come in, but I don't. (Fortunately, Bill Pay has helped a lot of this; I now have an online "filing" system through my bank where I can download most bills paid; then I just have to go through the credit card and cash receipts for the items not listed there.)

So as someone who hates filing, I have a pretty good system going. It works. And if I need to find some piece of paper quickly, I can usually do it.

I consider the state of my file cabinets – all four of the glorious old beaten beasts – a victory over ADHD. Instead of towers of terror, they are pillars of organization.

Well, kind of.

Calendars & To Do Lists

Use a calendar app or day planner. In my case I use both; I like the appointments to pop up on my computer and phone at least half an hour before I'm supposed to be somewhere (it's saved me from missing many an appointment). Each morning, I check my Microsoft Outlook calendar and my physical planner to see what I have to do and where I need to go. (I use Outlook for its calendar, task bar, and contacts list; I update it daily and frequently sync it to my phone.)

Use a planner – I've used the same "brand" every year for almost 30 years! I use this one by Mixed Role Productions:

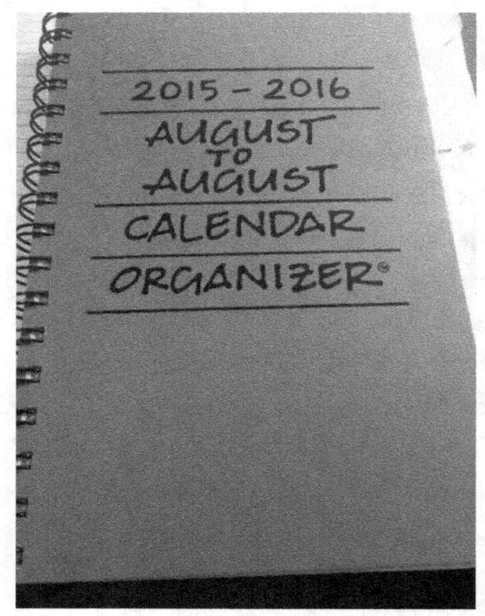

Make to do lists, and keep them where you'll actually read them. I know one epic fail is my to do lists. Oh, I'm great at keeping them…everywhere. On my phone, my computer, in my planner, printed out and hole-punched and put in my notebook, in a notepad next to my bed, on sticky notes everywhere, and even in a book of *To Do Lists* I designed. But then do I ever look at them and do them? Hardly ever, these days! So that is one of my next steps, to schedule in a "to do list" check a few times a week (I won't pressure myself with daily) and do a few. Just a few. Otherwise, it's too overwhelming. (After writing this, I switched to using "To Do" tabs in my Excel file, which is always open on one of my monitors. After I finish the task, I change the color to green. Done.)

I even created my own to do list book with categories.

Tackling To Do Lists

Let's face it, I'm good at making to do lists. They are everywhere: in my computer (Excel, Word, and Outlooks Task bar); on my iPhone (Wunderlist and various other list apps); in my planner; in my book, *To Do Lists: A book of lists for organizing & simplifying your life;* in my notebook; and in little notepads and scraps of paper.

Yep, I'm good.

Here's what I'm bad at: Actually doing them!

Oh, eventually, pretty much everything somehow gets done, but not in an organized, efficient way.

Do you know why?

Because I forget to look at my to do lists!

It definitely doesn't help to have them and not use them. Now, I have improved this system over the years so that there are certain, specific to do lists and items that I do right away:

- I pay bills and handle other paperwork (including adding to my to do lists, ha!) about once a week, when I take it all to a restaurant to sort through.

- I keep my work list Excel worksheet open at all times on one monitor, and as I finish a project, I change the text color to green for done.

- I keep a grocery list in my phone that I actually use, adding to it as I think of things, so I only have to go to the store once a week and not drive back for forgotten items.

So I am going to make a commitment to actually look at my to do lists, and do a few items every other day, or five days a week. Here is one item that's been in there for some time, but I keep forgetting to do:

- Make a dog-walking chart.

Now you'd think since I walk the dogs every day, I'd have this down, but every single time, I'm missing items I need. So here's my chart:

Dog Walking Chart

Bring:

- *Leashes*
- *Cleanup bags*
- *Bear spray*
- *Fog horn can*
- *Backpack with water*
- *Phone*
- *Treats*
- *Clicker*

There! It's done! Mission accomplished. Copied and printed and headed to paste it by the door, where the leashes hang. (Because if I don't do it now, I won't.)

The Magic of a Notebook

Keep a notebook. This saved my life in college. My grades were 1,000% (ADHD exaggeration time!) better in college than high school because I learned to use (1) a planner, (2) a notebook, and (3) syllabi.

How I wish middle school and high school teachers would give out syllabi. What a life-changer they were for me. I put every assignment due date in my planner and on my wall calendar. Then I knew when every test was and when every paper was due.

When I tutored college athletes during graduate school, I quickly learned the most important thing they needed to learn was how to make a notebook, organize their syllabi into it, and mark a calendar with due dates. Every week we'd check it and update it first.

When I taught college, I gave my students incredibly detailed syllabi, with a calendar, that showed every assignment right there for them.

What your notebook contains will vary with your own needs. I'm no longer in college and not working in an office, so it's changed over the years. But it includes the following tabs (I just fold over sticky notes; it's sloppy, but it works): Contacts, Computer Info, TOPS (a weight-loss support group I attend), My Son (school schedule, medical records), Medical (blood test results and other health information I might need), Voucher Records (for a nonprofit I volunteer for), Gym Schedule (in case I ever actually join a class), Calendar, and To Do Lists (of course). In the back is a nifty thing that holds my stamps and a pen, as well as folders titled "To Read" and "To File."

Manage Time

What a boring topic! Ha! So important, I know. But if I walked into a lecture hall where the topic was "time, work, and money," I'm quite certain I would sneak out before the bell rang.

So, I'll keep it short and simple – two of an ADHDer's favorite words!

Time management can be tough for ADHDers. In my case, when I'm working, it's hard to stop and do anything else, such as walk the dogs, take a shower, make something to eat, stretch my aching body, whatever. Probably what saved me from being a total workaholic (and killing myself with it) was having a child. Since I work at home, I could go all day and night working (and often did, actually). But once my son was born, I had to set a limit on my work schedule. I had many failures, even working two full-time jobs plus my contract work, somewhere in his first two years (I was desperate for health insurance) before I realized this was impossible. I remember saying to one of my bosses, "I have to give you notice. I need to go home and meet my son."

When my son reached school age, it helped me a lot. I now had a schedule. I tried to get everything done by whatever time my son got home from school, so he could have my undivided attention (well, as much as that is possible) the rest of the day and into the night.

So, by 3:00, I had to be done with work. Now, often, I had reports to edit and forms to make, so after he fell asleep, about 8:00, I went back to work. But at least he had me those 5 hours. (I wonder if he'll ever understand how hard and disciplined that was of me, and how much I loved him to do that – something so against my very nature. Well, at least I know you understand.)

Mainly, I learned to use the Microsoft Excel program in clever ways. For one thing, since I bill hourly, I'd note the time I started on a project, as well as every stop (that means every time I got up from the computer, because I might stop and do the dishes or whatever, and it didn't seem fair to charge a client for my ADHD breaks). I use the computer's clock to note the time.

Of course, I have been chronically late most of my adult life, except when teaching, thank goodness. I always felt stressed and scared like I was going to be late, but somehow I always slipped into the classroom right on the hour. Otherwise, I'm a mess.

I learned my lesson one day, years ago, when I walked into a doctor's appointment 15 minutes late, and the receptionist told me to forget about it! "We don't see people who come in late," she actually told me.

WTF! (That phrase wasn't used back then, though, so I actually thought "No f---ing way! You're kidding me!") I had just driven what should have taken about an hour to get here, but since there was a terrible snowstorm, the roads were icy and full of wrecks, so it took much longer. Now I had to turn around and go back home, another hour or two of driving, depending on the wrecks, and be scared to pieces the entire drive. For *nothing*! I was furious (as I should have been), but also ashamed (as I should have been). And forever after, I haven't been late to a doctor's appointment. (I actually prefer using the drop-in clinics now instead – problem solved.) If I have a 1:00 doctor's appointment, I get there at least 15 minutes and usually 30 minutes early, bringing paperwork, my phone, and whatever else I can to keep busy, distracted, and not bored.

I have a doctor who is chronically late with her appointments. I know that about her now, but I didn't know it then, and my patience wore out several times, so I up and left, bored to death, telling the receptionist I had another meeting to go to (lie). Now I know her, so I (1) make my appointment the first one after lunch (I could also do first one in the morning, but I'd never make it, so I don't), and (2) I bring at least 2 hours worth of paperwork to do. Everybody's happy.

The nurses and other staff sometimes apologize that she's taking so long, but I just sit in the waiting room and then the examination room all happy, buried in piles of paperwork and stupid phone calls to make, and say, "No problem; I understand what she's like, so I come prepared!" I actually look forward to it now as one of my Get All That Ugly Paperwork Done Days!

Have you ever missed an appointment because you can't find your keys? I have. Of course. So, I've learned to put them in the same place, every time (well, almost every time). And I keep a spare in the same place, a little plastic drawer on my desk, just in case I can't find the "main" one. Or in case I lock my keys in my car and have to call SO (yes, it's happened).

Do It Now

HelpGuide.org: advises "Deal with it now. You can avoid forgetfulness, clutter, and procrastination by filing papers, cleaning up messes, or returning phone calls immediately, not sometime in the future. If a task can be done in two minutes or less, do it on the spot, rather than putting it off for later." Personally, there are a lot of things I accomplish while on the phone. That's the time for no-brainer stuff, like hanging up clothes, folding towels, wiping counters, whatever.

Open the mail right away, tossing the envelopes and junk mail immediately, putting the other mail in my "to do" pile. I am great at this. It's become a no-brainer … pick up the mail and get it done. The End.

Historically, I've grabbed my "to do" pile of paperwork at least once a week, crammed it in a book bag, and go to a restaurant to do the dirty, ugly, nasty chore. But lately, with banking apps and better organization, I usually have my bills paid within a few minutes of receiving them.

File! I keep folders titled, "To Be Filed Files." Then twice a year, I'll go through and actually file them into the proper folders, so they are ready by the end of the year to go through for taxes. I keep empty folders in my notebook (which I always bring along on Paperwork Day at McDonald's (or whatever restaurant), so one folder is a new Records and Receipts To Be Filed folder.

12.   My Treatment Approaches #12: Purging & Donating

There are two issues at work in this treatment approach. Both involve getting rid of clutter because less clutter = a clearer mind and fewer distractions.

The first is purging, or actually throwing things away.

The second is donating, which feels good. The trick in either case is to let go.

Garbage Day

Garbage day is my favorite day of the week. It's when I get to get rid of a lot of stuff. I feel a general sense of dread if we don't have at-home garbage delivery, or if I'm not up in time to get the can out.

SO wanted to just keep the garbage here, hanging out in the garage, until he had enough to fill his truck, and then take it to them dump. The idea made me sick. I couldn't explain it well. We tried it for about a year, a year of numerous arguments over when he was going to the dump. There was never enough garbage for him; there was always too much for me.

Maybe it's my ADHD, but I like my weekly "appointment" to get the garbage out.

Since tomorrow is garbage day, today I will go through and empty all the bags in all the trash containers, empty the cat litter entirely, clean the yard (dogs, remember?), and start with a fresh week. It feels good, like starting anew. (I also take recycling in on Saturdays, now that we finally have it where I live.)

Donating

Donating feels both bad and good. I never regret it after; I'll say that. Sure, it might be hard to let go of things, but those are fewer things I have to clean, sort, move around, and worry about. Let someone else deal with them. A home with less clutter and more space is easier to clean and easier to live. I believe it makes ADHD much less of a "problem."

Books

The hardest thing for me to get rid of is a book. I love books. I love the look of them on a shelf and the feel of them in my hands. I used to (and I still do with many) hang onto books desperately, as if my life depended on them, regretting any I loaned because they never came back.

But then I had an epiphany one day. Most of the classics I love are free online. And almost everything else I can get at the library. For free. (And the librarian gets to deal with the organizing, dusting, and clutter!) Also, I don't reread books anymore like I did as a child (I read *The Call of the Wild* at least 10 times). There are so many wonderful books to read and a short lifespan to do it in. So I can pass on many of my books to thrift stores.

Cry a little here. Okay, done.

Games & Toys

When I look at the stacks of games I have purchased for my son, most of them still unopened, I get mad. We've argued about them numerous times. I'm upset because he wanted them (especially the expensive ones like Settlers of Catan in all its various forms) and promised he'd play with them, but of course he doesn't. It's not entirely his fault, I know, since he doesn't have siblings and his parents don't play board games. But on the other hand, he has had a few friends over since getting them, but they only want to play Minecraft on the computer.

So looking at the games makes me upset. And why keep something that makes you angry? Especially at your beloved child? It's really not his fault. At all.

So I am going to get rid of the games, maybe box up the ones that are precious to him like Catan, but get them out of my sight, at least. Most of them I'll donate so that someone else's children can enjoy them.

Goodbye puzzles and games. (I moved many of them to the garage shelves just in case he finds a friend who loves board games.)

Linen & Towels

I can't seem to get a sheet that stays on my bed. Whether it's my weight (can't be?) or the three or four dogs that hop up in bed with me, my sheets pull out. I try various brands that say they'll work, but none of them do.

Finally, I go to a mattress store and get what works. I should have done that in the first place.

Now I have about five sets of king-size sheets that I don't use. But I can't get rid of them. They can work on my son's full-size bed. They can work on the guest bed. They can! It's too much money. I worked hard for it, and I can't just give them away!

Or can I?

And what about towels? I do have quite a few. It's not like I wasted money on them; most of them were my mother's, so they are at least 20 and probably more like 30 years old. (It's amazing how well they've held up.) I am quite certain I don't need a Sponge Bob beach towel, though.

Time to give away. Last fall, I discovered that animal control uses towels and blankets in the cages for the poor dogs and cats to sleep on (thank God they do; most shelters don't – convince them to if you can), so I didn't feel badly about giving away some of our precious linens to them.

I can give away more. I have enough.

Electronics – Especially Cords

Why can't the telephones, DVDs, computers, backup drives, GPS, cameras, CD players, TVs, radios, speakers, Blue Ray players, fax machines, Fitbits, iPads, cell phones, and all the other electronics we have running our lives use the same cord? Same type charger?

It drives me crazy!

So many stupid hours of my life I've wasted trying to match up cords and items. I've put stickers on them, used the plastic tags from bread on the cords to mark what they go with, taped items with like cords, whatever. It's still always a pain.

It seems easier just to get rid of the items. And their ridiculous cords.

In fact, I did that one day …just took an entire file cabinet drawer filled with cords and chargers and bagged it and gave it to a thrift store. Haven't missed one yet, and it's been a year!

"Dust Collectors"

I went to visit my friend P, and I was stunned with how immaculate her house was. But I also felt like I was in a hotel room (which is nice, actually). Something was missing.

Oh right, it's knick knacks.

Her shelves were completely empty and polished. Mine are rich with items such as plastic plants that look real, a duck collection of my father's, an elephant collection of my mother's, an antique clock, candles, and various other knick knacks that people have given me over the years.

"Why don't you have any knick knacks?" I asked her.

"Oh, do you mean dust collectors?" she replied.

I guess I do.

I think I have a few too many, but none is not enough. My sister, the hoarder, has been overtaken by knick knacks; it's possible she could be killed under the weight of them falling on her someday, or she could break a leg by tripping on them (and has, I think).

What is needed, I think, is balance. (I actually took pictures of some of those precious parental knick knacks and gave them to my brothers. Win-win.)

Paper & Paperwork

I have a paper problem. Meaning, I like paper. When I was a child, blank paper represented the world to me, as in the world I could create through stories and drawings. I loved writing notes and letters to people, also.

Over the years and moves, I have given away paper; it was probably the hardest thing to part with. But today I am parting with more.

I take the too-large paper I bought to copy nonprofit newsletters back when I had a copy machine and the various craft papers I bought for my son and put them in the Goodwill bag. Good, done, lots of space created. I didn't kill over and die getting rid of that paper. Sigh.

Next I go through my file cabinets and toss old receipt files I no longer need (over 3 years per IRS.gov; see references). That felt good too.

Then I switch my banking and investment accounts to e-delivery only, so I no longer have to worry about filing their stupid statements every month.

Office Supplies

It happened after my parents died. I was sitting in the downstairs rec room that I had converted to an office, staring at a paperclip. I'd been trying to work on a report, and I reached for a paperclip, and then it hit me:

"I have enough paperclips for the rest of my life."

Life is short. I have enough. I don't need to ever get another paperclip.

This is the kind of wisdom that hits you after those closest to you leave.

If ever I had a hoarding problem, it was with office supplies. Not only that, I had a theft problem. – not really intentional. I couldn't seem to get out of an office meeting or store without someone else's pen, as in, I always forget mine so I borrowed theirs, then threw it in my purse thoughtlessly. You know how your dentist or doctor's office has giant plastic flowers taped to the top of their pens? That's so ADHDers like me don't walk off with them.

So, I have enough pens. Enough pencils. Enough glue. Enough everything.

I had to try to explain this to my son a couple years ago when we got the school supply list. Of course, he wanted me to buy everything on it,; he thought he had to have it or the teachers would be upset.

"But you already have at least 50 colored pencils," I said. "I know, because I organized them right into your colored pencil drawer."

"But I need them. It says so."

Sigh. Okay, I'll waste more money and buy more stupid pencils that eventually I'll just give to Goodwill anyway, because you will grow up and go to college and leave me with thousands of pencils to remember you by.

I got distracted. Sorry.

The point is, I have a lot of office supplies, such as pens, and I also use a lot, but I will die long before I use them all. Time to purge.

Purging

ADHDers function better with less stuff. This certainly applies to me.

Fortunately, even though I hate wasting money and I get the little feeling of sadness when I first pick up something with the thought of getting rid of it, just like most of us do, I stuff it in the contractor bag and never miss it. And when I drop that full bag at a nonprofit thrift store, I feel good. I am happy to see it all go.

It feels good to get rid of stuff.

I think of it this way: if my house were to burn down, what would matter? What would I actually need? My family and my pets. That's all. What would I want? Photos, you'd think, but I had them all scanned and put them up on Dropbox, so I have them in case of disaster. No problem. My computer I would love to save, but since all my files are stored online, I can live without it.

So step #1 is purging, more and more purging, sharing the wealth of what I have (i.e., too much stuff) with others.

What is hardest to purge? Anything belonging to my son, even if he's outgrown it. Books. Magazines. Office supplies. Electronic toys (Kindle, DVD players, etc.). Anything I inherited from my parents. I thought the latter was impossible until I figured out the "trick" of handing them over to my siblings.

What is easiest? Clothes. I never did care about them. Still don't. I don't know why I carried around those size 8 clothes for 10 years after my baby was born; I didn't get back to that size (although I'm close now!), and they just made me feel bad. Finally, I told myself, "Look. If you lose that much weight to ever wear these clothes again, then you deserve new outfits. In the meantime, let someone else wear them." So there they went.

Hardest thing to purge in my life? Definitely my son's jogger stroller. I actually was holding onto it at Bishop's Attic where I was donating it, gripping harder as they tried to take it. It didn't just represent my entire son's babyhood and toddlerhood, but it also was my safety chair, my freedom. It was like my wheelchair. So with all my injuries, particularly the knee and neck, and then the fibromyalgia pain, I could take it to the fair, for example, and when I couldn't walk anymore, have an instant chair to relax in while my son rode rides. I could store my book bag underneath it and always have plenty to read (and not hurt my neck and shoulder worse by carrying it). I could put my coffee and coke in the plastic cup holders.

What I really wanted was to keep it for me, for all its practical uses, of course. And don't say "get a walker or a wheelchair"; those don't function like the jogger stroller. It was easy to push, even on gravel and steep dirt or snowy trails, and I could still get a good workout while using it, which is impossible with a walker (I've tried). It was the height of a shopping cart, which relieved the back pain … something to gently lean into.

So in my mind, a thousand times, I've invented a "sports walker" of sorts, for people like me, who like to carry their work with them and have an instant chair, but of course, I'll never be able to complete the design because of ADHD. (So if you know a great designer who wants to go into business together, email me!)

(By the way, I wonder if inventing things is part of the ADHD mind. I have invented or imagined things all my life; as a child, I used to write companies with my brilliant ideas even – almost all executed, although they'd write back and say things like, "Thank you; work is already under way for that product.")

13. My Treatment Approaches #13: Managing Work

Some of this was covered in Chapter 15 "Managing Distractibility," but work is so important to so many of us, that I am separating it into its own short chapter as well.

Work More Efficiently

I'm pretty darn efficient at work, I have to say.

As long as I don't' have to actually go to work.

I have set up my home office with all the "distractions" I need (i.e., four monitors) and don't need (a private office, with walls and a door; no other human beings in the room to chat with me; a phone I can ignore; a fax that is not plugged in; and especially, no meetings. I have cozy lamps for lighting; otherwise, I keep it dark and quiet.

I have tried and failed miserably at working in offices due to meetings (although using my grad school strategy of writing everything down to keep me busy and silence my ADHD blurts helps); fluorescent lights (distracting and the opposite of calming); people talking, visiting, cooking, eating, gossiping, and arguing (not a good environment for a writer/editor); and the worsening fibromyalgia pain from sitting at a desk for 8 to 10 hours a day. Then I have to commute two hours a day, back and forth to Anchorage, sitting again, in a car, bored (audio books help) and in pain. Then there is the guilt of being away from my son and dogs.

ADHD strategies that work for me: I keep the cell phone in my bedroom, away from my office, when I'm working. I don't have a television in my home office, or even a music player (except on my computer, which I don't use when I'm working). I have my books organized so I can easily grab the one I need if I'm researching that particular topic. I try to keep my planner open in front of my main monitor, so I daily look down and make sure I don't have anything pressing or an appointment. I schedule a dog walk early in the day (about two hours after starting work for the day) to clear my mind and settle the mutts, so I can focus.

When searching online, though, I found I can improve in a few areas. Per HelpGuide.org:

- *Set aside daily time for organization. Set aside 5 to 10 minutes a day to clear your desk and organize your paperwork. Experiment with storing things inside your desk or in bins so that they don't clutter your workspace as unnecessary distractions.*

- *Use colors and lists. Color-coding can be very useful to people with ADHD. Manage forgetfulness by writing everything down.*

- *Prioritize. More important tasks should be done first. Set deadlines for everything, even if they are self-imposed.*

- *Save big ideas for later. All those great concepts that keep popping into your head? Jot them down on paper for later consideration.*

Not that I'll ever look at those notes again. For example, just recently, in cleaning out my to do piles, I found about 10 pages of notes I took at a writers' conference last year. I've never looked at them since, but it kept me focused to take those notes. I have to say that was the least-boring conference I ever attended: I was fascinated by the topic and the guest speakers; the speeches were short and fast-paced, and I was okay. On the other hand, the last conference I went to I found myself overcome with boredom, so I kept getting up and walking around (getting my pedometer steps), checking my emails, texting, whatever, to pass the time. Do I think this was a bad thing to do? No, absolutely not. It kept me in the room (I stayed in back so I didn't distract others too much), and it kept me listening.

HelpGuide.org has some excellent suggestions for focusing, which I'm surprised to see I am already incorporating in my own life: writing things down and pacing. However, I need to add their third suggestion, which should help me keep focused on conversations:

- *Get it in writing. If you're attending a meeting … that requires close attention, ask for an advance copy of the relevant materials – such as a meeting agenda or lecture outline. At the meeting, use the written notes to guide your active listening and note taking. Writing as you listen will help you stay focused on the speaker's words.*

- *Move around. To prevent restlessness and fidgeting, go ahead and move around – at the appropriate times in the right places. As long as you are not disturbing others, taking a walk or even jumping up and down during a meeting break, for example, can help you pay attention later on.*

- *Echo directions. After someone gives verbal instructions, say them aloud to be sure you got it right.*

14. My Treatment Approaches #14: Handling Money

I'm a workaholic who has made a lot of money.

Three times I lost it all.

Once I lent it to a boyfriend, who took it all, plus ran up all my credit cards, and ran to his next victim. The second and third time were from investing in stocks: (1) by brokers, and (2) by me doing day-trading. In these cases, the idiot and her money were soon parted. Someone got that money, but it certainly wasn't me. I took the last of my inheritance and safely stuck it in a company that I figured would last forever, Kmart, and then never looked back, hoping for the best. Until I saw on the news that Kmart declared bankruptcy, and my last dollar was gone for good.

Kmart did just fine, leaving broke souls like me scattered around the world while they reorganized and Sears bought them out.

I hate stupid bankruptcy. I hate investing. I hate stockbrokers.

It took me a lot of years to trust one, and now I do. He's helped me "wisely" invest the 15 years of 80-hour weeks trying to earn and save money again, although just a few days ago I called him all excited. "I want to buy some Fitbit."

Silence.

"It's really cool, and fun, and I just got mine and love it. It's a great product. What do you think?"

"I don't think it's a wise investment." But he agreed to put "a little" money in it.

A day later I read an online article that warned not to buy Fitbit.

I suck at investing money. I am not going to call my broker with any brilliant ideas again.

Turns out, I'm not the only investment idiot in the world. It seems to be pretty common with ADHDers.

I have, forever, found some tricks that work for me, and I researched what works for others, so here we go. I'll keep this short and sweet, because, after all, we both have ADHD, and money matters bore us.

First of all, what has saved me the most time and eased my stress the most are two things:

- Smile.amazon.com (I use smile to login so a percentage of my purchases goes to charity) – I get what I want, when I want, for free shipping to Alaska. I get exactly what I want (chewable vitamin D3 tablets; vegan chocolate mocha powder for my coffee, a tall nightstand with four drawers – things I could drive around spending hours searching for and not find).

- Using Microsoft Excel to keep track of my invoices, spending, tax records, and work to do. HelpGuide.org recommends using Mint and Manilla to monitor your finances:

    Once you've linked your accounts they automatically update. Manilla consolidates your statements and bills from all of your accounts into one place. Mint tracks all of your bank account and credit card transactions, and also offers budgeting and other financial analysis tools. Both tools can make your financial life easier.

- I try to just keep two credit cards, but then stores offer me a discount if I get theirs, so I end up with dozens. The last time I tried to cancel one, they talked me into keeping it another year; I don't know how that happened (I'm a phone-call failure, anyway; so how I handled this after writing this item was to cut them up and send the companies a good old fashioned cancellation letter – back to two cards). Anyway, simplifying is best for ADHDers, and especially if you have a problem overspending (many of us do due to impulsivity),

- Note: Through writing this, I discovered a much simpler way of carrying money and cards. I ordered a wallet case for my phone, put in the few cards and ID I need, and never carried a purse again. Whew! What a relief.

- Online banking has simplified my life. I downloaded my bank's app to my phone, and paying bills is so much easier now. Mobile deposit is also such a relief for ADHDers. I open the mail, find a check, get out my phone, log in, take a picture, and am done.

- Sticking to your shopping list and avoiding places where you overspend are recommended by HelpGuide.org.

15. My Treatment Approaches #15: Managing Changes

Like many ADHDers, I don't handle change well. Moving, packing, and vacationing can all be overwhelming tasks. Here's some of the issues and how I have learned to handle them.

Moving Furniture

One of the hardest parts about all my physical injuries (neck, shoulders, knee) and ailments (fibromyalgia, arthritis, spinal stenosis) was that I could no longer move furniture. And although I have a strong man in the house who could do it for me, he has absolutely no understanding of why I need to change things around once in a while. So it's not worth the days or weeks of begging and being told, "Just put it where you want the first time and leave it there."

So everything stays in the same place.

But this rearranging furniture is part of my being.

As a child, I had one glorious little room, and numerous books, aquariums, a bed, a nightstand, a desk, and some bookshelves.

I would draw out my plans for how I wanted to rearrange things, and then I would set out to do it. Probably four times a year.

The interim, as I moved, was sheer chaos, and I hated that step. I had too many clothes and books and such piled on the floor. And it took a long time to move things, especially because of the aquariums. They required emptying and heavy lifting. But when it was all done, and everything was put away and neat, I was happy. I love the feeling of diving into a perfectly organized, neat little room.

It was my spot of control in a house of chaos, where my mother hoarded.

Now, some days I think, I'd like to move this or that here or there, but then I think how I physically can't, and how SO doesn't understand how organizing the house organized my brain.

Packing a Bag or Suitcase

Traveling is hard work for someone with ADHD, especially the preparation. I have taken many trips, but it is always chaos, misery (for me and anyone with me), stress, and panic. All that equals major anxiety attacks.

"Take a chill pill!" my sister screamed at me once, and she was kidding, but I pulled out my (usually saved for midnight) Xanax and did.

One time I went to Europe. I'll probably never go again. It was too overwhelming, even though (maybe because) I went with a friend who is an accountant and the complete opposite of ADHD ... to a fault. There is no room for any change in her preplanned schedule. So when we got to the Coliseum in Rome, and she was ready to leave, telling me we had completed our allotted time there and needed to move on to the next stop, before I'd even browsed the bookstore, I said, "No more. You go without me."

She was furious; I was furious.

An accountant and an ADHDer. Not good traveling partners.

Actually, if the travel arrangements had been left to me, (1) we never would have gone, and (2) if we did manage to get somewhere, I'd never leave my hotel.

For me the best vacation in the world is to take three suitcases full of paperwork to a hotel room and take two or three days to get it all done. All the hundreds of articles various people (okay, my sisters) send me to read that I never have time to read, all the tax filing and organizing, all the "miscellaneous to be read and filed" batches, all the "to do" piles. Read, tossed or filed, and done. When I go home, two of my suitcases are empty.

Sigh.

My sister travels with me every time I go somewhere; she'll meet me and my son. I don't know if she'll ever do it again after last year's trips to New York City and Boston. She said she could see the city life beating down on me very physical presence after just a few days, and I said, "That's exactly how I feel inside, like a turtle pulling into its shell and hiding." Big cities don't just annoy me; they terrify me.

I needed a lot of chill pills.

The highlight of my trip was tripping on a hole in the sidewalk and lying in the hot sun crying, while New Yorkers (and even my own son and his friend) stepped over me.

I wasn't just crying because my knee hurt. I wanted to go home, crawl in bed with my dogs, and be where life makes sense, because I shaped my little cave to fit my personality. I know where everything is ... most of the time.

However, as a frequent traveler, I have learned a few tricks. One is that I get my suitcase out at least two weeks before a trip, and leave it open someplace obvious, like on the couch in my bedroom. That way when I suddenly think, "Oh, I should bring this or that!" I actually toss it into the suitcase. It takes me two weeks to pack, but I end up with everything I need.

Another trick is that I keep a makeup bag packed at all times ready to throw into the suitcase. It has shampoos, lotions, toothpaste and toothbrush, a comb, floss, and all kinds of other things that I might need or might not. (I like this kind so much, I also got one for electronic cords and chargers for traveling.)

Sometimes, just going someplace in the car can be overwhelming. For example, if I'm taking the dogs, I should have leashes for all of them, water, water bowls, bear spray (I am in Alaska, after all), "poop bags," treats perhaps, maybe a whistle (let's face it, that's never happened). But usually I end up with five dogs and one leash and a couple poop bags. I keep reminding myself to pack a backpack with all those things, but I never do. I forget that I was going to do that until next time I am with five dogs in the car.

Just now, I actually packed a little bag for a dog obedience class for one of the puppies. I think I actually did the packing (and instructions printing) because I'm trying to get my son to be in charge of the puppy in the class, not me. It is a five-week class, and I just finished doing one with the other puppy, but I never remembered one thing, except doggie treats.

My son's bag, now, just packed by me, has poop bags; two bags of dog treats; a blanket for the dog, two types of toys for her; a fanny pack for my son to wear to put the treats in; and whatever else the teacher asked for in the instructions. When it was all packed and done, I looked at it with a feeling of victory, kind of like getting a college degree. "Wow, I did that!" I thought. That was huge for someone with ADHD!

Returning from Vacation

I have the same mentality when I come home from a vacation, whether it's a weekend away or weeks away. I have to immediately empty all my suitcases, put my clean clothes in the closet, my dirty clothes in the washing machine, my makeup bag in the bathroom, etc., and get those suitcases empty and stored out of site that same night.

I think this is a good thing about me.

Moving

I have moved four times in the last seven years, and each time was always so stressful I think I'll never do it again.

The worst was the last one, because I had to empty out two houses entirely and quickly to get them ready to sell, with no time to sort and donate. So all the crap ended up here at my home. (Which is one of the reasons why I take weekly bags to donate.)

But as much as I hate moving, I'm really good at it.

What I do is, I unpack everything right away. I mean, the first day! And I put it all up. Sure, if you look at my bookshelves for the first few months (or years) after a move, the books are not in order and some are even upside down. But they are up. And not in boxes.

If you look in my cupboards after a move, you'll see nothing but chaos. But slowly, then, as the years go by, I tackle a specific task. Maybe it's a file drawer. Maybe it's moving some of the books so they are together with similar books. Maybe it's putting all the dog supplies in one drawer, the exercise equipment in another, the socks in one, the soups in one cupboard, etc. Although I moved here three years ago, none of these tasks was accomplished until this year.

That's the hard part about moving for me. Going back in and reorganizing.

16.   My Treatment Approaches #16: Managing Impatience

Okay, impatience is my worst ADHD trait. I can't put a good spin on it and tell you how it makes me a better, more unique person. When it comes to impatience, I'm a bitch and an asshole. Which makes people treat me worse. Which makes me depressed and hate myself. There's nothing good about it. And my worst place for ADHD impatience? No question: the telephone.

Telephone Fail

Studying ADHD has not helped my telephone skills. Let's give, for example, my vision of hell, trying to reach someone at "Obamacare," or healthcare.gov, who actually knows what they are doing. When I originally tried to apply for insurance, my son kept getting kicked to Medicaid, which we are not eligible for, so the system would not allow me to register. I cannot tell you how much dozens of hours of frustrating calls, day after day, week after week, month after month, this involved. The problem was in the computer program, but no one would believe me. I turned to write letters instead, but that just elicited a return call by someone who had no ability to help. Finally, months past the deadline, in which I ended up buying separate insurance for my son and myself, I found someone who figured out that yes, I was right, there was a problem in the program, and they actually used my "case" to try to fix it.

Have they fixed it? Not really. The same thing happened this year, so I figured out myself how to bypass the glitch by increasing my income and removing his social security income (since his dad is retired). I probably pay more for insurance, but at least I *got* insurance.

So 2 months ago, I receive a letter from healthcare.gov saying to call them. I'm thinking, "Why can't I mail you a letter instead like you did to me?" but I try the dang phone call. I was transferred to three different people, had to explain the reason for my call (which I don't really know) three times, and then they say they'll call me back in "5 to 10 days." That excruciating call took about 45 minutes and accomplished nothing.

God, I hate the telephone.

I didn't always hate it, but I sure do now. I don't think it's me that's changed; it's customer service that's changed. There is no one to answer calls, first of all, as you have to go through listening to long messages and click the correct number, over and over, to reach someone, who then transfers you to someone else, and on and on, and nothing is done.

I miss letters.

Today, as I'm headed out to walk the dogs, Healthcare.gov decides to finally call me back.

"Hi, I'm returning a call you made to healthcare.gov," the woman says, pleasantly enough, but it's what she said that riled me.

"I was merely making a call in response to your letter; if you don't know what the letter is about, then you're wasting my time."

Not nice, Jory, I know, but first of all, they are 6 weeks behind schedule in returning the call that I didn't want to make in the first place.

"Oh, I know what it's about. But I'm going to need some information from you."

I know she's about to start into a long spiel of questions that they already know the answers to, and the dogs are looking at me eagerly, wondering why we're not out the door yet, when I've already put on my coat.

"Well, I'm walking the dogs now, so if you can't be quick, you'll have to call back."

"You can call us back," she said.

"Well, that will never happen," I say, hanging up.

The call has upset me. I think, I should have explained why my calling her back would never happen. Because I have ADHD? Because I'm tired of wasting hours calling an agency or business that never knows what it's doing? Because she's 6 weeks late? Because they can't just say in the letter what they want? Because she wants to ask me a dozen questions before she'll talk to me? Because she's treating me like I need her, when really, according to the letter, she needs me?

Who cares? I'm out the door, walking the dogs, in nature, starting to breathe again.

Ok, I care. A little. I hate the bitch I am on the phone during these kinds of calls.

I come home and listen to the phone messages, which I haven't done in a week because I read it so much, and each time someone starts talking,

"Hi, this is the bank," I click and delete. "Hi, this is Jack," I click and delete. I don't bother listening to the rest of the call. I just delete six calls, impatient, miserable, hating the phone.

I wouldn't even have a home phone except that the ISP requires I buy a phone line in order to have Internet. More stupidity.

But I decide to go ahead and research how ADHDers can improve their phone patience, since clearly this is an issue for me.

It sounds bad and much bigger than the mere phone:

> *To interact effectively with others, an individual must be attentive, responsible and able to control impulsive behaviors. Adults with ADHD are often inattentive and forgetful and typically lack impulse control. Because ADHD is an "invisible disability," often unrecognized by those who may be unfamiliar with the disorder, socially inappropriate behaviors that are the result of ADHD symptoms are often attributed to other causes. That is, people often perceive these behaviors and the individual who commits them as rude, self-centered, irresponsible, lazy, ill-mannered, and a host of other negative personality attributes. Over time, such negative labels lead to social rejection of the individual with ADHD. Social rejection causes emotional pain in the lives of many of the children and adults who have ADHD and can create havoc and lower self-esteem throughout the life span. (NRCA, Social Skills)*

Hmmm. I can't control my behavior, am perceived by others as rude, and so I have low self-esteem. That's all pathetically uninspiring.

Honestly, I think I just want to stop answering the phone or listening to messages altogether. Maybe I can turn off the answering machine. Then people will be forced to write to me.

I have actually told three clients, who wanted to discuss everything that needs to be done with major projects over the phone, that it is best to email me, because I comprehend the written word better (and in my own time, plus I can refer back to it). It turns out that was a good solution; they seemed to understand and accepted it.

I didn't even know this was an option till one of my subcontractors said she couldn't do phone interviews with clients (I was trying to pawn this nasty task off on her). Wow! So I'm not the only one! I took great comfort in that, and have used her line since.

"I'm sorry, I don't work well over the phone. Can you email me, or write me a letter, please?"

I am going to practice this line, and I'm going to use it. I think I'll start by mailing a letter back to healthcare.gov and tell them just that.

But first I have to call Verizon and find out why my cell phone bill is skyrocketing. (It's not because I eve ruse the phone for phone calls, I can guarantee that!) Grrrrr.

Mood Problems and ADHD

So like most adult ADHDers, I'm moody, it turns out. As Asherson explains:

> *Mood problems are very common, with a constantly unstable mood that fluctuates up and down from moment to moment throughout the day. One person described swinging between the "fog" of a distracted mind and the "fire" of irritable and angry moods. Individuals with ADHD are frequently impatient, cannot wait for anything and become easily frustrated or irritated. As a consequence, they often avoid situations where they may have to wait their turn such as supermarket queues*

Well, that's distressing. But true. And getting worse as I age. Maybe because I've lost hope in life getting better? Life meaning the life going on in my very-active and constantly whirring brain.

I am "high maintenance," I suppose, because of ADHD. I know that I'm a pain in the ass for anyone in customer service, but mainly for anyone in customer service on the phone. Or in line.

Yesterday, for example, I was in a long line at the fair to get my son a lemonade, and a girl inched her way right next to me. I watched her with absolute hatred as I knew what was coming, and it did. When it was my turn, she stepped up instead, as did her friend who suddenly appeared.

"Really rude," I mumbled, but that's all I did. What else are you gonna do? Blow up? Cause a scene? Ruin everyone's day? Embarrass her and yourself?

Maybe, I tell myself, she thinks she was here first. Maybe it doesn't really matter in the scheme of things. Maybe my son will get his lemonade anyway, just a minute later than hoped for. Maybe, life will go on in spite of this incredible setback. Maybe I should just breathe. Deeply and slowly. And think of my father's words: "Let it go."

So I did that. And I survived. And I didn't make a scene.

So it's all good, right? Then why do I remember it, and with such distaste and still some anger? That's a shame.

Mood Matters

After reading about ADHD and mood swings, depression, anxiety, anger, etc. etc. I must say I don't feel very hopeful or good about myself. I see a pattern, flying back at least 30 years, of being tortuous to be around. I see, today, a 55-year-old lady who ruins people's day.

Crap.

How awful.

Okay, so we step forward by forgiving ourselves first.

Then we learn ways to fix it.

Managing Impatience and Boredom

There are ways to manage impatience. Look online for inspiration. These come from HealthCentral.com (Matlen, "Hate Waiting?"):

1. *Acknowledge that it's part of having ADHD.*

2. *Always come prepared! Bring activities to keep you busy when you know you'll be waiting for an appointment, traveling, etc.*

3. *See it coming and have a plan. If you're prone to car rage, practice the habit of deep breathing during stressful episodes. Switch the radio to a classical station. Keep a squishy fidget ball handy when stuck in non-moving traffic.*

4. *If you must partake in a boring activity, like a children's game, set a time limit for yourself. Play, then find another activity that you can engage in while still staying near your child; something akin to parallel play: knitting, playing a handheld video game, working on a crossword puzzle, etc. You may not be able to play with your child for long periods of time, but you'll still be close by and can chat with him about what he's doing.*

5. *Have fidgets on you (or if the case may be- your child) at all times. Squeeze balls are a great item to have. Spin rings help adults get through boring business meetings. You can find a large assortment of fidgets at www.myADDstore.com .*

6. *Chewing gum can help tremendously. If your child has a hard time sitting through a movie, or attending in class, offer gum. If the*

teacher protests, have a discussion about sensory needs and how chewing helps many to pay attention and self-calm.

7. *Personally, I have a very tough time sitting in a car for long. One hour is about my limit. Take turns driving. If you're the passenger and you're prone to carsickness, purchase or rent books on tape. Otherwise, bring reading material and a DVD player. Since I'm unable to read or watch movies in cars, I bring a notebook and write down ideas for articles or projects. I also bring a compact camera and look at the scenery as a professional photographer might. This gets me out of my own state of boredom and forces me to see "the ordinary" with fresh eyes.*

8. *While waiting for appointments, flights, etc., I always bring a mini laptop. These are so tiny, they can fit in a large purse or a backpack. Besides writing, you can play games or go online if you're lucky enough to hook into an internet connection.*

9. *Do conversations bore you because the speaker spends an endless amount of time going into detail and not getting to the point? Make a mental game out of it. Try seeing how much you can remember of the story being told. Visual cues are usually helpful, so pay close attention to the person's mouth. You'll have a better chance of staying connected. Ask questions, which will help you stay connected and focused.*

10. *If you're a student or in a business meeting, there's nothing wrong with doodling on your notebook paper or agenda.*

17. My Treatment Approaches #17: Winding Down

Creating a Space

My bedroom is my happy place. It is big, square, and a little too stuffed with couches and beds for the dogs and a rocking chair for SO. But those are practical things. It is, basically, my living room, my sleeping room, my TV room, and my calm place.

One of the ways that I have made it relaxing and "warm" for my soul, my ADHD personality, is through lighting. I don't use overhead lights; instead, I have a few warm lamps with golden lampshades, a string of Christmas lights on one wall, and a string of fall lights (soft greens, yellows, and oranges) on the other. I like to light candles and close the blackout curtains and make it what SO calls my "cave."

It's nice to have a space. If you can make one room your own, your little oasis from stress and worries, consider doing so. One of the most important thing I did was banish the computer from it. Computers mean work, fretting, checking, distractions. It's a good idea to leave the phone out too (I have one in my room, but I keep the ringer volume off.)

Why I Like *Columbo*

Calming Sameness

Most nights, I just want to crawl in bed and watch *Columbo*, who always comforts me. I can read and do puzzles and play with my iPad while his voice soothes me in the background. No need to actually "watch" or listen to *Columbo* ... the plot is always the same, and he always gets his man, or woman, so I don't have to actually listen.

In other words, it's the perfect show for someone with ADHD.

You'd think an ADHD mind would get bored with the same show on over and over, and it's true that many shows do bore me. I get up and walk around and take multiple breaks and pause the DVR and do a hundred other things during many TV shows and movies.

But I can put on *Columbo* and actually calm down, even – eventually – fall asleep. I don't really watch it, of course. I do other things, many other things. But Peter Falk's voice comforts me and calms my anxiety.

There is another show which relaxes me in much the same way as *Columbo* does; it is called *Murder, She Wrote*. Once again, the plot and main character is always the same. There is a beautiful consistency to it. I don't have to pay attention – like I did when I watched *Lost* or *Breaking Bad*, having to constantly pause them every time I needed a TV break (which is often, since I can't focus that long).

With *Murder, She Wrote* and *Columbo*, I can leave the room. I can fall asleep. I can check my phone, play with my dogs, talk to my son. I can read and do puzzles. I can be my ADHD self.

Does Columbo Have ADHD?

I wrote how I work things out when I'm doing my daily walk in the woods and let my mind wander where it wants to go. Just now, I figured out something else about Columbo.

The character of Columbo has, or pretends to have (it's never certain), ADHD.

"Just one more thing." This could be the ADHDer's motto!

Just like Columbo keeps coming back to pester people with his "just one more thing, sir," I state something, then think of something else, then another thing, and oh yes, there's this thing.

For example, to my son, on Sundays, which seems to be his only day he has any chores: "Don't forget to clean up the dog yard."

"I know!" Now he's distracted me. I fumble off, like Columbo, out of his room, where he's the computer, playing that darn child-sucking game

Minecraft, again.

Then I pop back in. "And be sure to empty the garbage bags on your way out."

"I know!" Glaring.

"Because it's garbage day tomorrow."

"I know."

I leave, then come back. "Be sure to fill up your bathroom garbage bags; I already emptied it, and there weren't any bags."

He ignores me completely now, not bothering to take off his headphones.

"And don't forget we have dog class tonight, so you should practice with Harper." (We both already know he won't. I'll have to do it, if it's to be done at all. But I can always hope. He's supposed to be in charge of his puppy, like I was the other one's class and training.)

He sighs and finally gets up, as if he's going to actually do those things, just to get away from me.

Like Columbo, I am irritating and constantly thinking of just one more thing. In his scatterbrained dialogues, he gets to the core of the problem, but brings up a half dozen other things that drive others mad. Here are some Columbo sayings that ADHDers can relate to:

> *I worry. I mean, little things bother me. I'm a worrier. I mean, little insignificant details – I lose my appetite. I can't eat. My wife, she says to me, "You know, you can really be pain."*
>
> *I gotta take off this coat. I can't think in this coat ... THE COAT, I can't think in the coat.*
>
> *She's mad at everybody. She's even mad at the ice cream man. "Why does the ice cream truck have to come just before lunch or just before dinner, spoil the children's appetite?" I have to listen to that. I hear that 3 time a week, you know that's 12 times a month.*
>
> *I don't thinks it's proving anything Doc, as a matter of fact I don't even know what it means. It's just one of those things that gets in my head and keeps rolling around in there like a marble.*
>
> *Well she was never exactly thin, I won't let her. I happen to like a woman ... well that's something else.* (Columbo Quotes)

Then there's the constantly fidgeting, looking for things, not being able to find a pencil or his notepad.

And there's the distractibility factor. How he'll be asking the killer (he always knows who it is, but pretends he doesn't) a question related to the crime, but then starts talking about food, or his wife's brother, or his uncle, or his dog.

So ADHD.

And he's, of course, a genius too. As his perp says in "Fade in to Murder:" "Listen Columbo, just for a minute how about we stop pretending that I'm brilliant and you're simple!"

So perfect.

No wonder I love Columbo so much.

He is me.

Other Relaxation Tricks

Overhead lights, especially fluorescents, have always bothered me. As a child, I remember not being able to concentrate on my reading or television viewing because my mom had the overhead light on in the dining room. I require the warm lighting of lamps. I also, for a few a hours a day, am okay with opening up the curtains to natural lighting. But no overheads, ever!

In the same way, I can't work in cubicles. I find the voices of other people and the thought that they can "spy" on me at any time distracting and upsetting.

Once I could afford it, I hired a housecleaner, and it really helped change my life so much for the better. I felt like it was a selfish thing to do ... I should be able to clean my own house for gosh sakes! But knowing someone is coming, particularly the same time every week, and handling the vacuuming and mopping and dusting, makes me feel able to breathe normally. It is like walking into a hotel room after the maid has come and fixed your chaos. I love it.

Sleep is absolutely necessary, but like many ADHDers, I'm an insomnia. Therefore, I take a sleeping pill to conquer the constant thoughts that I must do this or that. But I'm working on other strategies, such as listening to calming audio books at night instead of television and reading on the iPad or phone (the bright screen keeps me awake). Since I quit smoking, I'm trying to remember to do deep breathing once in a while; that seems to help calm me as well.

If you suffer from anxiety, and I have suffered from it, there is medication to help you. It's the one medication I absolutely believe in, but only when I'm trying to wind down and go to sleep. It calms my ADHD constantly running mind.

My problem is shifting from work and the "million" things to do to s state of relaxation.

Other than the anxiety medication, there are a few other tricks that have worked for me:

Do a Sudoku puzzle.

Do a crossword puzzle.

Find a television series on Netflix or DVR (so no commercials) that actually keeps your interest. (Or one that doesn't, but calms you like soft background noise, as I use *Columbo*.)

Read Facebook posts.

Use computer or iPad games like Minesweeper or Solitaire or Words with Friends, but only if you can limit them to a certain number of games or time (15 minutes, say).

Put things down on a to do list and wall calendar, and then let it go until tomorrow. It'll wait.

18. My Treatment Approaches #18: Interpersonal Relationships or Social Skills

Does Donald Trump Have ADHD?

This is the hardest chapter to write, and my biggest problem.

I'll start it by talking about Donald Trump. Because that makes sense, right?

Lately, no matter what your politics are, I've been listening to Trump try to run for president, and "flap his yap" inappropriately on almost a daily basis. As I listen to him refuse to apologize, or seem genuinely confused on why people misunderstood him, I wonder about him. For example, the word "whatever" might have been to him was a shift in thought, focus, and ideas, but it was pretty shocking to hear:

"You could see there was blood coming out of her eyes. Blood coming out of her wherever."

This morning, I was listening to him ramble on, fast and furious, his mouth unable to keep up with his brain, his words a jumble of ideas, trying to say that he meant "whatever" as it in "next topic" but refusing to apologize, and on to about 20 other topics in a few minutes, including personal comments about the people he mentioned (e.g., he said Chris Wallace is "a small shadow of his father" in the middle of saying something else), and I think: "Oh. Donald Trump has ADHD."

I'm no doctor or psychiatrist, of course, but doesn't he sound like one? The way he moves, how his words are brash, and the state of his desk in photographs (papers stacked everywhere in cluttered yet organized chaos – Google Donald Trump at desk). The way he has had multiple failed relationships. The foot in mouth disease. The hyperfocus that makes him successful; the jumping around from idea to idea that perhaps fails him or makes him fail in some ways (I'm not sure he's actually a success as much as he says; perhaps he's in tremendous debt). The ability to delegate to others is probably his best asset, and what has saved him from himself.

In any case, there is something about him that reminds me of me, the way I'm so opinionated and mouthy and frankly rude in my interruptions sometimes.

Crap. That's embarrassing. I have seen the enemy, and he is me? I have looked into his soul and seen a reflection of myself?

I – have – a – problem. I am the *creator* of problems!

I feel a little pity for Trump, suddenly, surprisingly. But do I feel pity for himself? No. Instead, I feel sorry for those who've suffered through my ADHD all these years. Especially SO. But also just about anyone whose every known me.

On behalf of myself – and Donald Trump although he'd probably call me a "fat pig dog" for saying this – we're sorry, people of the world.

Time to get busy working on this part of me that I've so ignored and defended, and maybe I have a chance to heal my current and past relationships a bit, as well as make for better future ones.

Handling Everything *But* Relationships!

What matters most to me is not how I feel, but how I make others feel, specifically, my SO, my son, my siblings, and my friends. And then, of course, there are the potential friends, or strangers.

ADHD has affected all of my relationships all of my life. It's too late to go back and change the times I ignored my parents, when they needed me, because I was hyperfocusing on work, holding too many jobs and writing too many reports. It's too late to visit my godmother again; the last time I did, down in Oregon, I only saw her once, then spent the rest of the week in the hotel room editing a 500-page proposal.

Sorry Nana.

But it's not too late to change how I relate to other people in my life.

So the purpose of this section is to figure out how to do so.

The first exciting thing I learn is that if both partners spend a little time learning about ADHD, they learn ways to understand, communicate, and respond to each other better. It's the "respond" part that I like. I am so fed up and tired of the stupid fights, the arguing over nothing, especially the way *he* gets all fried and angry because I interrupt or faded away.

I of course refuse to let him "win" an argument, not only because I'm ADHD, but because I was in an abusive relationship before, and I will not give up one iota of my power ever again.

So we are at a tense, panting, standstill of swirling anger and frustration.

Sick of it.

As I read about ADHD's role in creating havoc in relationships, I have an epiphany of sorts: Even during the 45 years before I was officially diagnosed with ADHD, I found and used strategies that managed my ADHD in almost all areas of my life – work, home, college, paperwork, organization, clutter, shopping, etc. – **except** personal relationships!

I never thought I could be to blame, or ADHD could be a problem, there.

Foolish me.

Improve the Marital (Significant Other) Relationship

So, I always thought it was him. Or them, as in any relationship I've been in. Sometimes it is. But the common denominator is me. Turns out, all this time I've been feeling the stings and arrows of his criticisms, being hurt, angry, and defensive, I was experiencing something common to ADHDers. As HelpGuide explains:

> *No matter what you do, nothing seems to please your spouse or partner. You don't feel respected as an adult, so you find yourself avoiding your partner or saying whatever you have to in order to get him or her off your back. You wish your significant other could relax even a little bit and stop trying to control every aspect of your life. You wonder what happened to the person you fell in love with.*

But in researching ADHD, you start to look at it from your SO's point of view. It's kind of shocking to think he's feeling "lonely, ignored, and unappreciated." That's not what I meant at all, but I can see that. Especially since we even live in separate spaces, rarely joining together, even to read or watch a show together. I wonder if he is lonely? (I have my five dogs and my son in my space, so I'm good.)

> *The non-ADHD partner complains, nags, and becomes increasingly resentful while the ADHD partner, feeling judged and misunderstood, gets defensive and pulls away. In the end, nobody is happy. But it doesn't have to be this way.* (HelpGuide)

Is This Relationship Worthy of the Work?

I like the idea of "transforming" my relationship with others, especially my SO and my son. Educating myself on ADHD is the first step in making drastic changes in how we all communicate and regard each other. Per HelpGuide, the answer is in understanding how ADHD symptoms are stressing and affecting us, then learning to manage those symptoms. (And my SO is supposed to learn to "react to frustrations in ways that encourage and motivate your partner" – good luck with that. I think the transformation is all on me, but I'll try to communicate it to him.)

I certainly know what upsets him most about my personality – how I don't listen to him. Everything else he can handle, but not that. It infuriates him. He takes it as personal rejection. He yells. I hate him for that, as it's just part of my being, my ADHD being, plus, as I said above, it's part of my keeping a sense of power in this relationship, from going to the horrible place where the abused woman lives (been there; will never be there again).

Not that he's abusive but being yelled at is still wrong, even if it's just for a few minutes here and there. But still. Wrong.

The reason I know it's not abusive is because I don't fear him. Not a bit. And I've lived in fear before in two relationships before: one because he was physical abusive and that threat of being hurt was always there, the other because he was downright crazy and even put a loaded pistol to my head.

Not good.

And yes, my SO is worth keeping, worth putting some time into improving our communication skills, since generally we are a good, solid, even happy couple, except that we can't talk to each other! Minor problem, right?

ADHD Symptoms That Cause Relationship Troubles

Here are the ADHD symptoms that can cause relationship trouble, per HelpGuide, along with my own experience; you can substitute "him" with "your partner":

- Trouble paying attention, as in I fade away when he's talking (frustrating to him, makes him feel "ignored and devalued").

- Forgetfulness. Maybe I promised something that I don't remember later (makes him "feel like you don't care or you're unreliable").

- Poor organizational skills. "This can lead to difficulty finishing tasks as well as general household chaos," says HelpGuide. "Partners may feel like they're always cleaning up after the person with ADD/ADHD and shouldering a disproportionate amount of the family duties." I don't think this one applies, especially since we live in separate parts of the house now (a duplex). Plus, being a woman, I think it's the opposite: I am expected to handle making all appointments and travel plans, shopping, raising the child, walking the dogs, scheduling repairmen, whatever. I have felt incredibly overwhelmed by having to handle not only my schedule, but everyone else's (soccer games, basketball practices, acting camp, dentist appointments, etc. etc. etc. till I want to scream, especially because no one else in my house bothers to accept the emailed reminders I send them to add to their smartphone calendars, look at calendars, keep planners, or help me in these tasks. So a few years ago, I started shoveling certain tasks to my SO, such as grocery shopping, making him to do lists of his own, and shifting many of the "driving our son somewhere" duties over to him. That helped cut down on my resentment a great deal. Of course, this only works when he is not working. Since he works construction, it's sporadic, and mostly summers only. Last winter, he had no work, which meant I got to actually get enough hours sleep a night to function while he took our son to school every day. It was blessedly wonderful. For me, as a controlling ADHDer, it is hard to trust someone else to actually do what needs to be done, but I have learned to let go, because I'm busy and overwhelmed enough already. Now if they would just learn to use a calendar!

- Impulsivity. The ADHD tendency to "blurt things out without thinking" can destroy relationships, as I well know from lost friends and family members. It can also lead to overspending. Since I support myself and work hard to make enough to keep us all happy, we're good there. However, I am slowing down, my income has dropped dramatically over the last 2 to 3 years, and I've let my family know that I'm no longer going to work myself to death, so they can stop expecting things like pool tables and new computers for Christmas. Less stress for me, and they seem fine with it, surprisingly.

- Emotional outbursts. Okay, I might be one of those

ADHDers who has "trouble moderating their emotions," but I had different techniques than the most common one listed by HelpGuide: "You may lose your temper easily and have trouble discussing issues calmly." No, instead, I turned to food (anything chocolate) and cigarettes to throw my anger into. Which meant I got fat and unhealthy. Now, I don't have food or cigarettes to hide behind. Since giving up sugar and cigarettes, I find myself much more angry than I thought I was; I knew I using them to "cope" but I didn't know how much they helped still my temper. My SO noticed, actually mentioning, "You sure curse a lot now." That was several months ago; I think it's winding down, especially since I've increased my exercise. But I'm ashamed to admit I used the F word. This summer. A lot. Fuck. I mean, fudge. I'm working on it.

How the ADHDer's Partner Feels

I guess it's hard for me to care about how my partner feels. My mind is so busy with a gazillion thoughts about how I feel. But for the sake of our relationship, I try to squeeze room in there for him. The main solution per "Adult ADHD and Relationships" isn't helpful to me at all. It sounds like torture:

> *The best way to put yourself in your partner's shoes is to ask and then simply listen. Find a time to sit down and talk when you're not already upset. Let your partner describe how he or she feels without interruption from you to explain or defend yourself. When your partner is finished, repeat back the main points you've heard him or her say, and ask if you understood correctly. You may want to write the points down so you can reflect on them later. When your partner is finished, it's your turn. Ask him or her to do the same for you and really listen with fresh ears and an open mind.*

Well, that's not going to happen, I'm quite sure of it. I can't stand listening. I suck at listening. Especially to him about how I upset him! Ugh! Yucky! To many ADHDer, that sounds like misery feels.

Maybe I can find another way. Perhaps, my trying to see ADHD through his eyes and understanding how my ADHD behavior makes him feel will keep me from overreacting to his criticisms. We're in a "Mexican standoff," though, as far as the power in this relationship goes. I want *him* to see *my* perspective more than I want to see his! But per Orlov, here is how the ADHD's partner may feel:

- ***Unwanted or unloved.*** *The lack of attention is interpreted as lack of interest rather than distraction. One of the most common dreams is to be "cherished," and to receive the attention from one's spouse that this implies.*

- ***Angry and emotionally blocked.*** *Anger and resentment permeate many interactions with the ADHD spouse. Sometimes this anger is expressed as disconnection. In an effort to control angry interactions, some non-ADHD spouses try to block their feelings by bottling them up inside.*

- ***Incredibly stressed out.*** *Non-ADHD spouses often carry the vast proportion of the family responsibilities and can never let their guard down. Life could fall apart at any time because of the ADHD spouse's inconsistency.*

- ***Ignored and offended.*** *To a non-ADHD spouse, it doesn't make sense that the ADHD spouse doesn't act on the non-ADHD partner's experience and advice more often when it's "clear" what needs to be done.*

- ***Exhausted and depleted.*** *The non-ADHD spouse carries too many responsibilities, and no amount of effort seems to fix the relationship.*

- ***Frustrated.*** *A non-ADHD spouse might feel as if the same issues keep coming back over and over again (a sort of boomerang effect).*

How the ADHDer Feels

One way that is helping already is providing my SO, and my son, with a little information about ADHD every day, as I learn about it. It seems like everyone is more relaxed, and they aren't constantly criticizing me for not paying attention. There's a tense quietness about the house, as if everyone is waiting to see where this journey takes me, how I come out of it, if the monster inside my head is cured.

I wonder too.

This little list might be helpful to show to my SO (or yours). The ADHDer might feel, per Orlov:

- *Different. The brain is often racing, and people with ADHD experience the world in a way that others don't easily understand or relate to.*

- *Overwhelmed, secretly or overtly. Keeping daily life under control takes much more work than others realize.*

- *Subordinate to their spouses. Their partners spend a good deal of time correcting them or running the show.*

- *Shamed. They often hide a large amount of shame, sometimes compensating with bluster or retreat.*

- *Unloved and unwanted. Consistent reminders from spouses, bosses, and others that they should "change" reinforce that they are unloved as they are.*

- *Afraid to fail again. Anticipating this failure results in reluctance to try.*

- *Longing to be accepted. One of the strongest emotional desires of those with ADHD is to be loved as they are, in spite of imperfections.*

Being Responsible

So what have I learned? I am supposed to "take responsibility" for my role in creating the dynamics of this relationship with all its woes. I was hoping for a better solution than that, something that didn't involve my taking any responsibility, but okay. Makes sense. Turns out, we both need to do a little work here (good). Both need to learn to respond to one another's concerns with consideration of their differences.

What the Non-ADHD Spouse Can Do Differently

I like the suggestions that the ADHDer's spouse quit nagging and yelling; I'll be sure to pass that on to my SO. Per "Adult ADHD and Relationships," the non-ADHD partner should follow these tips:

- *You can't control your spouse, but you can control your own actions. Put an immediate stop to verbal attacks and nagging. Neither gets results.*

- *Encourage your partner when he or she makes progress and acknowledge achievements and efforts.*

- *Stop trying to "parent" your partner. It is destructive to your relationship and demotivating to your spouse.*

- *Develop a routine. Your partner will benefit from the added structure. Schedule in the things you both need to accomplish and consider set times for meals, exercise, and sleep.*

- *Set up external reminders. This can be in the form of a dry erase board, sticky notes, or a to-do list on your phone.*

- *Control clutter. People with ADD/ADHD have a hard time getting and staying organized, but clutter adds to the feeling that their lives are out of control. Help your partner set up a system for dealing with clutter and staying organized.*

- *Ask the ADHD partner to repeat requests. To avoid misunderstandings, have your partner repeat what you have agreed upon.*

What the ADHDer Can Do Differently

But then, I have work to do also, it turns out, sadly:

- *Acknowledge the fact that your ADHD symptoms are interfering with your relationship. It's not just a case of your partner being unreasonable.*

- *Explore treatment options. As you learn to manage your symptoms and become more reliable, your partner will ease off.*

- *Find ways to spoil your spouse. If your partner feels cared for by you — even in small ways — he or she will feel less like your parent.*

- *To improve communication, do what you can to defuse emotional volatility. If need be, take time to cool off before discussing an issue. When you have the conversation, listen closely to your partner. Ask yourself what you're really arguing about. What's the deeper issue?*

I have suggested to my SO that we might benefit from couples counseling and therefore learn better ways to manage my ADHD and his way of reacting to it (i.e., arguments!).

"Do you really want to spend your Golden Years fighting like this? Because I sure as heck don't!" I said.

He continued to argue about whatever it was we were fighting about (it was in the car, of course; he was driving, so maybe it had something to do with that, but honestly, I've forgotten), ignoring my counseling suggestion. I tried to push it a few more times, but he continued to ignore me, which is his way, I suppose, of saying no.

We definitely need to learn how to communicate better.

The next Treatment Approaches chapter focuses on listening skills, or communication tips. Of course, this applies to all relationships, including the spousal one, but I thought it important enough to deserve its own chapter.

19. My Treatment Approaches #19: Improving Relationships through Listening Skills

As I read about ADHD and consider my failed relationships and friendships over the years, particularly my role in causing tension in my family, I realize there is much still to discover. Specifically, I make it my mission to work to improve the following relationships:

- My Significant Other (SO)
- Children (not just mine, but all children), siblings, and other family members
- Friends
- Work associates and meeting attendees
- People on the telephone
- People that serve (such as store clerks, bank tellers, and waitresses)

These are all areas where I need improvement. But key to most of them is my being a better listener, which most of all means being "present" in the conversation. This is so easy to say, but it is overwhelming to think of putting it into practice; controlling the ADHD mouth and thoughts is the key to most of our issues, isn't it?

Still, there are always strategies worth trying. The following are some of the strategies I've learned in my research:

- Try to focus my racing mind so I don't jump in with interruptions; especially try not to jump ahead in my thoughts to what my next sentence is going to be! ADHDers tend to blurt out what comes to our minds immediately, as (in my view) we are afraid if we don't, that thought will be lost forever. **Well, it might be; it might not; does it really matter?** Or is listening to what the other person says more important?

- Look people in the eye from time to time; I especially avoid eye contact with strangers (clerks and waitresses).

- Like Columbo, keep a notepad handy (and like Columbo, I'll probably keep losing it and my pen), especially for meetings, writing down what is said to keep me paying attention.

- If I lose track of what people say, maybe admit this, and ask for a repeat of their key points. Maybe to slow, rambling talkers, admitting that I am having difficulty focusing will guide them to stick to the point.

- Many sites and books recommend paraphrasing what someone said to you back to them, to help keep you in the conversation. I can see this as a potential way of my interrupting again, but it's worth mentioning.

- I like the suggestion of Tartakovsky (in "How Adults…"), who suggests the ADHDer "visualize the story" by making a kind of game of it, playing out what the person is saying as a movie in your head: "Imagine all the colorful details." That might work, keeping my thoughts busy and my mouth shut!

- Use fidget toys. As mentioned previously, I ordered fidget toys of various sizes; keeping a small one in my pocket to have handy might help me focus. I can also use a squeeze ball or Play Doh.

- When friends are over for long visits, having a dog on my lap or near me to pet, scratch, and groom works the same as the fidget toys, only the dog gets a great happy benefit of hours of my attention. The same idea will work with a cat, of course, as long as they are patient enough to let you play with them.

- "Keep your advice to yourself" says Maynard. Wow! That's so not me. I always assume that the *only* reason anyone even talks to me is that they *need* my esteemed opinion! But of course, most of the time, people just want to talk, "explore their thoughts and feelings," and my tossing in opinions and advice is deadly to the conversation. I am shocked that I have been misunderstanding this my entire life.

- Let people know when I am "hyperfocusing" on work, so I can't pay attention right now. Sometimes my son or SO is talking to me while I'm working on a report or book, and I'm saying, "Um hmmm," as if I'm listening to him, but of course I'm not. For some reason, I thought I was, all these years, but then they'll say later something like, "I already told you that!" and I'm quite sure they didn't. It's almost always when I'm working, my thoughts deep in the hyperfocus state, room for nothing else. Hyperfocusing while working is my favorite time as far as my mind is concerned, because the dozens of "other" thoughts and ideas are stilled, the past and future worries and regrets have faded away, and all I think of is the task at hand. I think this is probably how "normal" people think – one thing at a time. It's nice. But no, I can't listen to you when I'm working. I'm in the zone; I'm gone to anything else.

So I've thought of a strategy. The next time they come in to tell me something, I'll ask if they can wait a few minutes. They'll probably get mad at this, request, pout, leave the room, saying, "Never mind!" in frustration. How do I know this? Because they've done it to me a hundred times before. Then I can't concentrate on my work, so I follow them, begging them to tell me what they wanted to, but they refuse, as a way of punishing me. God, I hate ADHD, but more I hate other people's misunderstanding and reaction to ADHD, taking our distractions so personally.

So, I've thought of another strategy (we ADHDers are good at thinking up new ideas, anyway!). I'll just have to learn to stop, pull my fingers away from the keyboard, turn around and face them, look them in the eye, and pay attention! Maybe I'll grab my notepad and write down what they are saying. This is a genius solution. I think I can do it.

I just hope I can get back to hyperfocusing on my work as needed, afterwards. If I can't, and I find it ruins whatever job I am trying to finish (usually on deadline), I'll have to try a sit-down meeting with the family and explain the problem to them and ask them for solutions. One that I hope to come from this conversation is that they won't get upset if I ignore them, that they won't punish me by refusing to talk to me when I do pay attention, and that they won't get hurt and mad at me for this "flaw" in my personality, but instead will understand.

- On a related note, sometimes when my son has something he needs, I'll ask him to write it down or to text me. So two nights ago he came home from school and said, walking by, "I need a graphing calculator, T184C." Ha. "I'll never remember that," I said, "can you text it to me? And your dad?" He texted it to me only, of course, so the next day I set out to find the beast. Of course, the first store was out of them, but I had them call the other store (10 miles away) to hold one for me, and they did. I confirmed the number on the calculator packaging with the number on the text, and yay! Task done. Easy peasy. In the same way, I put a magnetized to do list on the refrigerator, and I have my son write down what he's running low on, so I have a list to grab for the store. Or, he'll text it to me.

Good ole HelpGuide offers some communication tips specific to a spousal relationship that I thought relevant; some are redundant, but they are the ones worth repeating:

- *Find the humor in the situation. Learn to laugh over the inevitable miscommunications and misunderstandings. Laughter relieves tension and brings you closer together.*

- *Listen actively and don't interrupt. While the other person is talking, make an effort to maintain eye contact. If you find your mind wandering, mentally repeat their words so you follow the conversation.*

- *Ask questions. Instead of launching into whatever is on your mind — or the many things on your mind — ask the other person questions. It will let him or her know you're paying attention.*

- *Request a repeat. If your attention wanders, tell the other person so as soon as you realize it and ask him or her to repeat what was just said. If you let the conversation go too long when your mind is elsewhere, it will only get tougher to reconnect.*

Lara Honos-Webb suggests some additional amazing strategies at Sharecare.com; I love every one of these:

- Use deep breathing to help keep your mind focused, she suggests. This is a great idea; certainly, simply using deep breathing has helped me through panic attacks and quitting smoking, so why shouldn't it help me listen to some dull (or what I perceive as dull) discussion?

- Make it a game to "connect drifting thoughts to actual content" as in trying to draw mental lines between the distractions in your head and the words being spoken by the person you are trying to listen to. Basically, we are having fun with our ADHD here, using our amazing creativity to both go with the distractions and use them to be part of the actual spoken words going on outside our busy little minds.

- Pretend you are a reporter; you have to go back to the office and write an article about what the person said. Genius solution for someone like me! I can listen quite attentively when I'm interviewing someone for an article or book. I love this one! "Like a reporter," she writes, "get the information you need by asking who, what, when, where, and why."

- Imagine taking your emotions and sticking them high on a shelf where you can't touch them, until after you have listened fully when you are "distracted by your sensitivity to the other person's emotions or your own intense emotion." Another brilliant idea. I get so caught up in my opinions and passions – especially when they concern children and animals – that I interrupt, argue, get upset.

- Take pity on the other person instead of getting frustrated with them. For example, I am impatient with slow talkers and especially those who repeat things. It drives me ADHD mad! I jump in and finish their thoughts for them to get the hell of the conversation over with. Just feel sorry for them, she says. I think this is another good idea. I don't think I'd try to rush someone who was truly suffering or sick, so why not think of these people as that way, that they are suffering to get the words out (more than I am suffering listening to them).

- Finally, like many writers about ADHD, Honos-Webb suggests you repeat or paraphrase the person's words back to them to show you are understanding and involved, and to keep your focus on the conversation. I think of this as a useful idea in the way that a college English teacher changed my entire ability to read textbooks by giving the class a "trick," which I've used it ever after, even today, to mark up books. She said, "As you finish each page, write down a brief summary sentence or two up top." This was for a Shakespeare play, and her intent was so that we could quickly find the part in the play we needed during class discussions (i.e., "Romeo meets Juliet for the first time"). But for me it became a brilliant way of focusing my mind on the words on each page of whatever I was reading. So why not use this same idea in conversations? Listen so that I can summarize back to the speaker. Brilliant!

I feel more confident now about my listening abilities. I am excited to try out these ideas, and see if my relationships with others change for the better. I have a feeling they will. I added these key ideas to a new list in the Wunderlist app, to review before the next visit with friends or family members.

PART TWO:

THE JOURNEY'S END…
AND BEGINNING

20.   My ADHD Adventure: Applying What We've Learned

Self-Help Is Key

We ADHDers are smart. We have a lot of brain activity going on ... maybe too much. At least that's how it feels.

Fortunately, there is a lot we can do on our own.

We don't have to necessarily rely on medication, therapists, or physicians to somehow "cure" us, although they might be helpful. But even if we do take these routes, ultimately, it is up to us to self-educate and apply what we learn. I am sure you agree with me on this, or you would not be joining me and reading my journey. As HelpGuide.org writes:

> *While it is true that there is no cure for ADD/ADHD, there is a lot you can do to reduce the problems it causes. Once you become accustomed to using strategies to help yourself, you may find that managing your symptoms becomes second nature. ("Help for Adult ... ")*

This is wonderful news! We can help ourselves. We know what the problem is; now we just need to use those incredibly smart brains of ours to figure out the best solutions for us personally.

What I've Learned about My ADHD

What I'm Good At

I am creative. This is not unusual with ADHDers. This is one of my new ways of seeing ADHD as a gift, not a curse.

I have developed some incredible organizing solutions over the years that help me not only function, but excel.

I am an amazingly hard worker, I'm honest (only charge for time worked), and I've never missed a deadline. I turn out quality work.

I can create many organizing tools I need on the computer (such as the medications and dog walking charts I made while writing this book).

I explored various apps and programs to help me organize my life better, and I found some to use (such as switching to an iPhone, which allows me to record verbal notes and messages, Wunderlist or similar apps for to do lists, etc.).

I have done a great job of *not* being a hoarder. There is always more I could donate, and more areas I could clean, but generally, I keep things put away and living space fairly clean.

I am a loving, caring person who is a pretty darn good mother and partner (could improve, I know), and an excellent pet "owner" (I don't like that term). I have rescued many dogs, and they have rescued me right back. I am open to their love and unique personalities, even my hot-headed "ADHD dog."

What I Need to Work On

I need to remember to look at my planner and to do list daily.

I should try to do and cross off several items on my to do list a day.

If there are things that have been on my to do list for years, and haven't been accomplished, it might be a good idea to just delete them permanently, and "let it go."

I have created many of the problems I have with interpersonal relationships. Therefore, I aim to try to the following:

- Listen better

- Be more involved in family activities and conversations

- Plan and hold more family activities (such as game night)

I should especially try to see things from my partner's point of view. He is not my enemy. Maybe I've just made him feel like he is.

I am still overwhelmed by paperwork, but I've committed to a weekly goal of going through the stacks and filing, tossing, or dealing with them.

I think I will always panic during tax preparation (and that's just getting everything ready for my accountant!). But by using Bill Pay for all bills, filing, and an annual file review and Excel list of purchases and expenses, it is doable, and not as time-consuming as it used to be. I might be able to find better fixes in the future.

I started scheduling in daily showers. Otherwise, I get started on the computer and then dog walks and then and then and then's…and I forget. Or I delay, because I think I'll get all sweaty from the dog walk, and I really should go to the gym first (but I don't), or maybe I'll vacuum first (but then I don't), or I am going to treadmill (nada). Turns out I'm not the only ADHDer who can "forget" to pay attention to personal hygiene (brushing teeth, showing). (Check out addforums.com if you think you're alone on something; it's amazing to read how many others are just like you!)

I need to calm down and enjoy life more.

I need to stop thinking about the negatives (such as how the trails are going to be turned into landfill instead of enjoying them now as they are).

I need to work on my worrying and anxiety, especially about my son.

I should be nicer on the telephone, particularly with strangers.

I want to improve my relationship with my siblings.

I find it hard to break away from work (or even reading, which is why I read fewer novels than before) once I'm hyperfocusing on a task. I need to learn to set a timer and once it goes off, get up and take a break.

I am good at picking up things, doing laundry, doing dishes, putting things away…but I don't think I'll ever be good at cleaning, especially floors. For this reason, I hire a housecleaner to come in once every week or two to keep my house sanitary (especially with five dogs and two cats!).

I have no patience for cooking, but perhaps there is a way I could change this up a bit. Slowly, I am learning to eat healthier, as I've become a vegan, and I make time every morning to make a smoothie, so perhaps I can also make time to prepare actual meals? Perhaps if I played soothing music (such as Gordon Lightfoot) in the background? Just a thought….

Although I'm great at keeping things hidden in cupboards, shelves, and drawers, I can always improve on organizing those spots. There is still a lot of "junk" in my junk drawers that I can live without. Purge! Donate!

I find that candles, warm lamps, and soft light strings (Christmas or fall colors) calm me. Right now I have them only in my bedroom, but perhaps I should incorporate them around my house.

I love music, but except for the car, I hardly ever play it in my house. I should make it easier for me to turn on some mellow music in the background while I work (perhaps too distracting) or least while I clean.

I tend to panic when I'm not in my self-created nest of space. Traveling can be fun for 2 to 3 days, but then I start to close in upon myself, overwhelmed especially by big cities and crowds of people. I need to find ways to improve upon this.

Similarly, I don't handle change well when it involves my routine. I even feel a sense of panic if there's an appointment change once it's "in" my calendar.

Maybe you, like I have done here, can make a list of your own strengths and weaknesses, and take that list to a counselor or give it to a friend or partner to work out strategies to address the "What I Need to

Work On" list. I am going to start by printing this list for my SO and I to go over together. I think it will help him understand me and perhaps open up communication.

Where I've Improved Since Studying ADHD

Studying ADHD has been so calming for me. I came to understand and forgive myself. I have been more gentle on me.

And I am surprisingly more tolerant of others. I realize that some of the symptoms of ADHD I've seen in others – actors I don't know, relatives and friends I do – used to bother me, perhaps because it reminded me of something troubling about myself. Now I get it. I mellowed a bit. I am a nicer person for this awareness and understanding.

I've also realized that there is no reason to get upset over menial tasks like having to make phone calls or fill out incredibly dull and tedious paperwork (such as the kennel license application I've been dreading and avoiding for six months but did yesterday in one fell 5-hour swoop [it required an evacuation and emergency plan that had me stumped]). It's just part of life, no matter how much I delay it, and it has to be done, so I find ways to get it over with sooner rather than later (no procrastinating). I find that making the dreaded phone call to ask a question or two can actually save me an incredible amount of time. (For example, I received in the mail a horrendous 15-page form to fill out yesterday, but a simple 5-minute phone call ended the need to fill it out.) And I find that actually doing the paperwork and getting it over with is much more fulfilling than filing it in some folder that is named "Stuff To Do," which I dread opening.

I'm much more empathetic to my son and my significant other since beginning this journey of discovering what ADHD does to me and to those who know me. I recognize my role in most of our family-related difficulties, and I'm happy to say as I've improved, so have they. We are getting along better, with fewer arguments.

I am more understanding of my son's challenges now. He had said he had ADHD after learning about it in school, and I didn't believe him, but now I see the things I got upset about regarding his not remembering to turn things in, not correctly understanding or writing down assignments, making careless mistakes, not paying attention to details, and especially, losing things show him to be a classic "inattentive type" ADHDer. I hope to help him with this, or get a therapist to do so.

What I Need to Appreciate

I've learned many coping skills over my lifetime of having ADHD, fortunately. But it was a long, slow process getting here.

Mostly, what turned my life around was finding a man I love and trying to learn how to get along with him (still working on that).

And even more was having a child. How much happiness and calmness being a mother has brought to my life (and sure, a whole new level of worry and anxiety too).

And, of course, how can I leave out the overwhelming pureness of being loved by dogs, so nonjudgmental and open?

I have much to be grateful for.

I am also grateful to ADHD.

"What did she say?" you might ask.

I am creative, hard working, able to juggle dozens of tasks at once, and overall amazing. Because I have ADHD.

Lucky me! Lucky all of us who are ADHDers!

Works Cited

+SupportGroups. ADD Support Group. Website accessed August 3, 2015: http://adhd.supportgroups.com/

ADHD Adult Support Group. *Facebook*. Website accessed August 3, 2015: https://www.facebook.com/AdhdAdultPage?fref=ts

"ADHD Diets." WebMD. Website accessed August 9, 2015: http://www.webmd.com/add-adhd/guide/adhd-diets

"Adult ADHD and Exercise." *WebMD*. Website accessed August 9, 2015: http://www.webmd.com/add-adhd/guide/adult-adhd-and-exercise

"Adult ADHD and Relationships: Tips for Developing a Solid Partnership." HelpGuide.Org. Website accessed August 5, 2015: http://www.helpguide.org/articles/add-adhd/adult-adhd-attention-deficit-disorder-and-relationships.htm

Ames, Jory. Birth 101: Reflections of a Reluctant Mother. Wordsworth LLC Publishing: 2014.

Ames, Jory. For the Love of Dogs: My Life in Dog Years. Wordsworth LLC Publishing: 2014.

Ames, Jory. Poor Little Allison: The Struggle to Survive a Loved One's Murder. Wordsworth LLC Publishing: 2014.

Ames, Jory. Quitting Smoking Diary with Activities Journal: 16 Weeks to Being Smoke-Free and Changing Your Life. Wordsworth LLC Publishing: 2015.

Ames, Jory. Quitting Smoking Journey: Changing My Life, One Cigarette and Story at a Time: A motivating, educational book to help you quit, forever.... Wordsworth LLC Publishing: 2015.

Ames, Jory. To Do Lists: A book of lists for organizing & simplifying your life. Wordsworth LLC Publishing: 2015.

Ames, Jory. Weight Loss Diary with Food & Exercise Journal: 16 Weeks to a Better Body. Wordsworth LLC Publishing: 2015.

Ames, Jory. Weight Loss Journey: Changing My Life, One Pound and Story at a Time. Wordsworth LLC Publishing: 2015.

Asherson, Philip. "Adult ADHD." BBC. *Science & Nature: TV & Radio Follow-up*. Website accessed September 2, 2015: http://www.bbc.co.uk/sn/tvradio/programmes/horizon/adhd_adult_qa.shtml

"Attention deficit hyperactivity disorder." *Wikipedia*. Website accessed July

30, 2015:
https://en.wikipedia.org/wiki/Attention_deficit_hyperactivity_disorder

Bailey, Eileen. "What Types of Exercises Are Best for ADHD?" *HealthCentral.* ADHD. April 23, 2013. Website accessed August 21, 2015: http://www.healthcentral.com/adhd/c/1443/160481/types-exercises-adhd/

Bennett, Jon. "L-tyrosine, missing in ADD-ADHD People." *3 Steps to Conquering ADD-ADHD.* Website accessed July 27, 2015: http://3stepsadd.com/premium/l-tyrosine-missing-in-add-adhd-people/

Centers for Disease Control and Prevention (CDC). *Attention-Deficit/Hyperactivity Disorder (ADHD).* Website accessed August 14, 2015: http://www.cdc.gov/ncbddd/adhd/diagnosis.html

CHADD: Children and Adults with Attention-Deficit/Hyperactivity Disorder. Website: www.chadd.org

Columbo Quotes. Website accessed August 9, 2015: http://www.columbo-site.freeuk.com/quotes.htm

"Comedian Rick Green shares his personal experience with ADHD." *YouTube.* October 16, 2013. Web site accessed August 8, 2015: https://www.youtube.com/watch?v=svjOT7Y2KYQ

DeNoon, Daniel J. "Can ADHD Be a Gift?" WebMD. Website accessed August 16, 2015: http://www.webmd.com/add-adhd/childhood-adhd/features/is-there-gift-in-adhd

"Don't Break the Chain' for ADDers." *Working with ADHD.* December 11, 2012. Website accessed August 21, 2015: http://www.workingwithadhd.com/dont-break-the-chain/#more-1618

"Good Stuff About ADHD!" *ADHD Centers.* Website accessed July 30, 2015: http://addcenters.com/kids/good_stuff.htm

Griffin, R. Morgan. "Adult ADHD Therapy: Finding the Right Therapist." *WebMD.* Website accessed August 9, 2015: http://www.webmd.com/add-adhd/features/adult-adhd-therapy-finding-right-therapist

Hallowell, Edward. "Worry Wart Remover: 8 Ways to Let It Go." ADDitude. Website accessed August 27, 2015: http://www.additudemag.com/adhd/article/8895.html

Hallowell, Edward M., and John J. Ratey. *Delivered from Distraction: Getting the Most out of Life with Attention Deficit Disorder.* New York: Ballantine Books: 2006.

Hallowell, Edward M., and John J. Ratey. *Driven to Distraction: Recognizing and Coping with Attention Deficit Disorder from Childhood through Adulthood.* New York: Touchstone: 1994.

Harding, Anne. "13 Tips for Buying Gifts for Children with ADHD." *ABC News.* Website accessed August 6, 2015: http://www.health.com/health/gallery/0,,20442916,00.html

Healthline. "The ADHD/Anxiety Link." Healthline.com. Website accessed August 27, 2015: http://www.healthline.com/health/adhd-and-anxiety#TheLink1

"Help for Adult ADD/ADHD." *HelpGuide.org.* Website accessed August 3, 2015: http://www.helpguide.org/articles/add-adhd/adult-adhd-attention-deficit-disorder-self-help.htm

Honos-Webb, Lara. Answer to "How can I improve my listening skills if I have adult ADD?" Sharecare.com. Living with ADD/ADHD. Website accessed August 21, 2015: https://www.sharecare.com/health/living-with-add-adhd/how-improve-listening-adult-add

"How to Know If You Have ADHD." By Nigahiga. *YouTube.com.* Website accessed August 8, 2015: https://www.youtube.com/watch?v=5GBMS7WPFSs

Iliades, Chris. "7 ADHD Stress-Reduction Techniques." *Everyday Health.* November 11, 2011. Website accessed August 6, 2015: http://www.everydayhealth.com/adhd-pictures/adhd-stress-reduction-techniques.aspx#01

"Impulsivity." Wikipedia. Website accessed July 30, 2015: https://en.wikipedia.org/wiki/Impulsivity

IRS. "How long should I keep records?" *IRS.gov.* Website accessed August 6, 2015: http://www.irs.gov/Businesses/Small-Businesses-&-Self-Employed/How-long-should-I-keep-records?

Jewison, Norman. Director. *Fiddler on the Roof.* Music by Jerry Bock (original musical) and John Williams (adaptation). United Artists. 1971.

Kessler, Zoe. "Class Clown: Why are ADHDers So Damn Funny?" *ADHD from A to Zoe with Zoe.* PsychCentral®. Website accessed August 8, 2015: http://blogs.psychcentral.com/adhd-zoe/2010/03/class-clown-why-are-adhders-so-damn-funny/

Lopez-Anderson, Kristen, and Robert Lopez. "Let It Go." From the album *Frozen.* 2013. Published by Wonderland Music Company. Label: Walt Disney.

Main, Beth. "ADHD and Obsessive Thoughts: Too Clingy, Insecure?" ADDitude.com. Website accessed August 21, 2015: http://www.additudemag.com/adhdblogs/11/9067.html

Mann, Denise.. "9 Steps to End Chronic Worrying." Health & Balance. *WebMD*. Website accessed August 27, 2015: http://www.webmd.com/balance/features/9-steps-to-end-chronic-worrying

Matlen, Terry. "Hate Waiting? 10 Survival Tips for the Bored and Impatient." *ADHD*. Health Central.com. February 19, 2009. Web site accessed September 2, 2015: http://www.healthcentral.com/adhd/c/57718/60050/10-survival-impatient/

Matlen, Terry. "Stop Obsessing! Taming the Worry Wart and Rumination." *ADHD*. Health Central.com. March 12, 2008. Website accessed August 6, 2015: http://www.healthcentral.com/adhd/c/57718/21417/stop-worry-wart/

Maynard, Sandy. "5 Ways to Listen Effectively with Adult ADHD." *ADDittude: Strategies and Support for ADHD & LD*. Website accessed August 21, 2015: http://www.additudemag.com/adhd/article/1988.html

McFerrin, Bobby. "Don't Worry, Be Happy." *Simple Pleasures*. EMI. 1988.

"Meditation for ADD: Techniques and Research Outcomes." *ADD-treatment.com*. Website accessed August 6, 2015: http://www.add-treatment.com/meditation-for-adhd.html

"Meditation Techniques: Adult ADHD & Mindful Meditation." *YouTube*. Website accessed August 6, 2015: https://www.youtube.com/watch?v=9Wxs_RQ9lZc

National Resource Center on AD/HD (NRCA). *Social Skills in Adults with ADHD (WWK15)*. Website accessed September 2, 2015: http://www.help4adhd.org/en-us/living/relandsoc/WWK15

National Resource Center on AD/HD (NRCA). "Succeeding in the Workplace (WWK16)." *Living with AD/HD: A lifespan disorder*. Website accessed August 26, 2015: http://www.help4adhd.org/living/workplace/wwk16

O'Neill, Eugene. *The Hairy Ape*. 1922.

Orlov, Melissa C. *The ADHD Effect on Marriage: Understand and Rebuild Your Relationship in Six Steps*. 2010. Plantation, FL: Specialty Press, Inc.

"Overview of Biofeedback." *WebMD*. Website accessed August 6, 2015: http://www.webmd.com/a-to-z-guides/biofeedback-therapy-uses-benefits

Pallarito, Karen. "15 Signs You May Have Adult ADHD." *ABC News*.

August 2, 2013. Website accessed August 6, 2015:
http://abcnews.go.com/Health/15-signs-adult-adhd/story?id=19844005#

Pera, Gina. "Finding ADHD in Fictional Literature." *ADHD Roller Coaster: News and Essays about Adult ADHD*. May 1, 2015. Web site accessed August 15, 2015: http://adhdrollercoaster.org/essays/finding-adhd-in-fictional-literature/

Preston, Tammy. "Mediation." *AdultADHD.net*. Website accessed August 6, 2015: http://www.adultadhd.net/meditation/

Previn, Andre G., and Dory Previn. "(Theme From) Valley of the Dolls." 1968. WB Music Corporation.

Raley, John. "Exercise: An Alternative ADHD Treatment." *ADDitude: Strategies and Support for ADHD & LD*. Website accessed August 16, 2015: http://www.additudemag.com/adhd/article/3280.html

"Ritalin." *Drugs.com*. Website accessed August 6, 2015: http://www.drugs.com/ritalin.html

"Sh*t no adult with ADHD says." *TotallyADD.com*. On *YouTube.com*. Website accessed August 8, 2015: https://www.youtube.com/watch?v=AeC040DqzFk

Sherman, Carl. "Is It Depression or ADHD?" *ADDitude: Strategies and Support for ADHD & LD*. Website accessed August 18, 2015: http://www.additudemag.com/adhd/article/748.html

Story, Colleen, and Rena Goldman. "5 Natural Remedies for ADHD." *Healthline*. February 24, 2015. Website accessed August 16, 2015: http://www.healthline.com/health/adhd/natural-remedies#Overview1

Tartakovsky, Margarita. "7 Tips for Dealing with Distractions for Adults with ADHD. PsychCentral®. Website accessed August 6, 2015: http://psychcentral.com/blog/archives/2015/07/05/7-tips-for-dealing-with-distractions-for-adults-with-adhd/

Tartakovsky, Margarita. "How Adults with ADHD Can Become Better Listeners." PsychCentral®. Website accessed August 21, 2015: http://psychcentral.com/blog/archives/2014/03/31/how-adults-with-adhd-can-become-better-listeners/

WebMD. "Vitamins and Supplements for ADHD." Website accessed August 25, 2015: http://www.webmd.com/add-adhd/guide/vitamins-supplements-adhd

Wurtman, Judith J. "Serotonin: What It is and Why It's Important for

Weight Loss." *Psychology Today.com*. Website accessed July 27, 2015:
https://www.psychologytoday.com/blog/the-antidepressant-diet/201008/serotonin-what-it-is-and-why-its-important-weight-loss

Wylde, Bryce. "The Dopamine Diet." *The Dr. Oz Show*. May 10, 2013. Website accessed July 27, 2015:
http://www.doctoroz.com/article/dopamine-diet?page=1

ABOUT THE AUTHOR:

Jory Ames, Ph.D., writes and lives in Alaska. She has taught college English throughout the Northwest and has been a successful technical writer and magazine editor for 23 years. She enjoys her family, writing, reading, music, nature hikes, mountains, dogs, and cats but is not so much a fan of cold Alaskan winters. Jory has been volunteering for humane societies since 1977, particularly focusing on ending pet overpopulation. She has published seven books and hundreds of poems, short stories, articles, and essays in newspapers, literary journals, and magazines.

NONFICTION

ADHD Treatment Approaches: How I Took Control
Birth 101: Reflections of a Reluctant Mother
Blank Weekly Calendars with To Do Lists
For the Love of Dogs: My Life in Dog Years
Just One More Thing: A Writer's Journey to Understanding and Managing ADHD.
Poor Little Allison: The Struggle to Survive a Loved One's Murder
Quitting Smoking Diary with Activities Journal
Quitting Smoking Journey: Changing My Life, One Cigarette and Story at a Time: A motivating, educational book to help you quit, forever....
To Do Lists: A book of lists for organizing & simplifying your life
Weight Loss Diary with Food & Exercise Journal: 16 Weeks to a Better Body
Weight Loss Journey: Changing My Life, One Pound and Story at a Time: Six Months to Wellness

POETRY

Lucifer and Other Love Poems
Poems of Love, Loss, and Regret

CONTACT THE AUTHOR:

I appreciate your reading my book. Here is how you can contact me:

- Visit my Website: http://www.joryames.com
- E-mail: jory@joryames.com